The Caucasian Chalk Circle

Works of Bertolt Brecht
published by
Arcade

The Caucasian Chalk Circle

Collected Stories

The Good Person of Setzuan, adapted by Tony Kushner

The Good Person of Szechwan

The Good Person of Szechwan, Mother Courage and Her Children,
and *Fear and Misery of the Third Reich*

Life of Galileo

Life of Galileo, The Resistible Rise of Arturo Ui,
and *The Caucasian Chalk Circle*

Mother Courage and Her Children

Mother Courage and Her Children, adapted by David Hare

Mr. Puntila and His Man Matti

The Rise and Fall of the City of Mahagonny and
The Seven Deadly Sins of the Petty Bourgeoisie

The Threepenny Opera

The Threepenny Opera, Baal, and *The Mother*

BERTOLT BRECHT

The Caucasian Chalk Circle

Translated from the German by James and Tania Stern
with W. H. Auden

Edited by John Willett and Ralph Manheim

ARCADE PUBLISHING • NEW YORK

FIRST ARCADE PAPERBACK EDITION 1994

The Caucasian Chalk Circle, originally published in German under the title *Der kaukasische Kreidekreis,* was first published in 1960 in this translation, which was revised in 1976 and 1984.

Library of Congress Cataloging-in-Publication Data

Brecht, Bertolt, 1898–1956
    [Kaukasische Kreidekreis. English]
    The Caucasian chalk circle / Bertolt Brecht ; translated from the German by James and Tania Stern with W. H. Auden ; edited by John Willett and Ralph Manheim. —1st Arcade pbk. ed.
          p.   cm.
    ISBN 1-55970-253-2
    I. Willett, John. II Manheim, Ralph, 1907 – . III. Title.
PT2603.R397K393   1994
832'.912 — dc20   94-2517

Published in the United States by Arcade Publishing, Inc., New York
Distributed by Little, Brown and Company

10 9 8 7 6 5 4 3

BP

PRINTED IN THE UNITED STATES OF AMERICA

CAUTION

Contents

Introduction

The Caucasian Chalk Circle is one of a group of plays which Brecht wrote during his six-year stay in the United States. He arrived on 21 July 1941, by ship from Vladivostok, after having set out from Helsinki two months earlier via Moscow and the Trans-Siberian railway. He left again by air on 31 October 1947, to return to Europe and in due course Berlin. Most of the time in between he spent living in the Los Angeles area where he had landed, though he also made prolonged visits to New York.

As in Munich nearly a quarter of a century earlier, his mentor in this new world was the now internationally successful novelist Lion Feuchtwanger, who persuaded him to remain on the West Coast where he would be close to Hollywood and its large German film colony, several of whom (like Fritz Lang and William Dieterle) were subscribing to the fund on which he and his family initially lived. Besides the three original plays and the adaptation already mentioned, his output in this period also embraced a number of rejected film outlines and synopses, including the story 'Caesar and his Legionary,' which was later taken into *Tales from the Calendar,* as well as an undertermined portion of the material for the film *Hangmen Also Die,* which Fritz Lang actually made. To this must be added the American version of *Galileo,* whose evolution is covered in the introduction to that volume, and a trickle of very fine but mostly rather short poems. His theoretical writing seems to have dried up almost entirely; major prose projects like the Caesar and 'Tui' novels went into cold storage; and he gave up writing short stories. So it is mainly on the contents of the present volume that his American experience must be judged.

To start with, its impact on his work was disastrous. This was due above all to something that had happened on the journey: the death of his aide Margarete Steffin in Moscow from tuberculosis. Both the group of poems which he wrote 'After the death of my collaborator M.S.' (included in *Poems 1913–1956*) and his own private notes and journal entries suggest that this was among the severest blows he ever suffered; a month later he could write commenting on it:

> for nearly a year i have been feeling deeply depressed as a result of the death of my comrade and collaborator steffin. up to now i have avoided thinking at all deeply about it. i'm not frightened so much of feeling pain as of being ashamed of the fact. but above all i have too few thoughts about it. i know that no pain can offset this loss, that all i can do is close my eyes to it. now and again i have even drunk a tot of whisky when her image rose before me. since i seldom do this even one tot affects me strongly. in my view such methods are just as acceptable as others that are better thought of. they are only external, but this is a problem which i don't see how to resolve internally. death is no good; all is not necessarily for the best. there is no inscrutable wisdom to be seen in this kind of thing. nothing can make up for it.

Very soon after arriving, too, he learned of the fate of another close friend, Walter Benjamin, who had killed himself on the French frontier in 1940 rather than risk being handed over to the Gestapo. At the same time, however, the atmosphere of southern California was hardly such as to relieve his depression. This was partly a matter of its utter remoteness from the war – 'Tahiti in urban form' he called it soon after arriving – though Pearl Harbor that autumn brought reality closer; partly a deep-seated resentment of its artificiality and underlying commercial ethos. Thus a journal entry of March 1942 (one of many to the same effect):

> extraordinary in these parts how a universally demoralizing cheap prettiness stops one from leading anything like a cultivated, i.e., dignified life.

On top of this came the often degrading experience of working for the films, which bore particularly painfully on him as he became drawn into the making of Fritz Lang's Czech resistance movie during the summer of 1942. Taking stock towards the end of April, he listed all the factors hampering him, from his loss of

Steffin to his lack of money, and concluded that 'for the first time in ten years I am not doing any proper work'.

Yet even while he was battling over that film (for adequate representation of the Czech people, for his theme song, for a part for Helene Weigel and a scriptwriter's credit for himself: on all of which points he failed), his outlook in other respects was beginning to improve. Materially, he and his family no longer had to live on $120 a month, but were able to move into a bigger and very much pleasanter house in Santa Monica (1063 26th Street; it is still there, though the area has been much built up) on the strength of the $10,000 which Lang got for him. Once again he was working with the composer Hanns Eisler, who had arrived there in April and for whom he now wrote his 'Hollywood Elegies', condensing much of what he felt about the civilization around him. He was also in touch with a young lecturer at UCLA called Eric Bentley, who differed from the bulk of his friends in being neither central European nor involved in show-business, and who seems immediately to have helped him to widen his English reading. From Feuchtwanger he heard that the Zurich Schauspielhaus wished to stage *The Good Person of Szechwan*, while Thornton Wilder had seen and been impressed by their production of *Mother Courage*. Still more changed for him when El Alamein was followed by Stalingrad (for it should never be forgotten how closely and continuously Brecht followed the war news). And during that October he and Feuchtwanger began collaborating on the war play, a modern Saint Joan story, which was to become *The Visions of Simone Machard*.

There followed his first visit to New York, which lasted from February to late May 1943, and which launched Brecht on the writing of *Schweyk in the Second World War* as well as on the first stage of *The Duchess of Malfi* adaptation. And then, around October, when *Schweyk* was still uppermost in his mind, Brecht went to visit Luise Rainer, who was living in Westwood not far from his 26th Street house, and without any personal acquaintance with him had signed the affidavit allowing him to come to the United States. She was then at the height of her fame after her performance in the film of *The Good Earth*, and as they were walking on the beach Brecht asked her what, of all plays, she would most like to appear in. When she named the *Chalk Circle* he instantly responded, for once again this was a theme which (as the editorial note will show) he had been taking up intermittently for several years previously; indeed he told her that he had suggested it in the first place to Klabund, whose adaptation had so successfully been performed by Elisabeth Bergner in Berlin in 1925. Miss Rainer in turn got in touch with a New York backer called Jules Leventhal, who was anxious to bring her to Broadway in a suitable work, and advised him that it would be worth commissioning Brecht and paying him a monthly salary till he had finished the play. This was formally arranged during Brecht's second New York visit, which lasted from mid-November to the middle of March. But he does not seem to have given Leventhal much information about his plans for the play, so that when the actress returned from performing to the troops in the Mediterranean she saw Brecht in New York to find out what was happening. According to her, he reacted so disagreeably as to make her call off her participation. None the less Brecht got down to the writing very soon after his return to Santa Monica, finishing the play in something close to its final version by 5 June, when he sent it off to her (so he noted in his journal). She was then ill with the after-effects of jaundice and malaria from her Mediterranean tour, and can no longer recollect its arrival. She was, however, aware that the play had developed an extra act since Brecht started on it, and that this was connected with his wish to give his friend Oscar Homolka a good part as Azdak, something that had not originally been bargained for.

In the meantime Brecht's financial circumstances, which nine months before had been very precarious, had changed as a result of the sale of the film rights of *Simone Machard* to MGM in February. This seems to have been due entirely to Feuchtwanger, who when Sam Goldwyn failed to understand the play got him to read the much more conventional *Simone* novel, buy the rights, and then buy those of the play as well. Brecht and Feuchtwanger had $50,000 to divide, in return for which there could be no stage production without Goldwyn's permission for the next three and a half years. Perhaps this is one reason why Brecht seemed so little discouraged by the collapse of the original *Chalk Circle* plan (which was not yet Caucasian when his journal first mentions it in March) as to carry his preoccupation with it right through the summer of 1944. Thus he reworked the character of Grusha, whose goodness, like Simone's patriotism, had seemed too arbitrary, and tried to make her tougher; he rewrote the prologue; and he asked his neighbour Christopher Isherwood to make a translation. When Isherwood refused it was arranged that James and Tania Stern should translate the play for Leventhal, with lyrics by W.H. Auden, who was sharing a house with them on Fire Island. (Part of their translation appeared in spring 1946 in the *Kenyon Review*, after which the script was lost, only to turn up ten years later on one of the microfilms deposited by Ruth Berlau in the New York Public Library.) By September he seems to have more or less finished the fully revised script, which was to remain virtually unchanged for the next ten years. That month his child by Ruth Berlau, called Michel like the child in the play, was born and died in Los Angeles. Coincidentally or not, he laid the play aside and by the end of the year was deeply involved instead in the *Galileo* project with Charles Laughton, who had recently become very taken with Brecht's work.

The Caucasian Chalk Circle was put on in America by students at Northfield, Minnesota, under the direction of Henry Goodman (subsequently of UCLA Drama Department) who had been bitten with Brecht on seeing the *Galileo* production of July 1947. This took place in May 1948 after Brecht had left the country, and used Eric and Maja Bentley's translation, which had at some point supplanted that by the Sterns and Auden. At Brecht's suggestion the Bentleys omitted all reference to the prologue, which led to rumours alternatively that they had suppressed it as too Communist or that Brecht added it later to give a pro-Soviet flavour to an otherwise delightfully unpolitical play. Two and a half years later, when Brecht was back in Berlin, he saw the Austrian composer Gottfried von Einem in Munich and tentatively arranged for a German-language première at the Salzburg Festival, to be directed by Berthold Viertel with Homolka as Azdak and Käthe Gold as Grusha. Though their plan never materialized, he managed to interest Carl Orff in the idea of writing the music: something that Hanns Eisler found uncongenial. This was partly because there was no real certainty of a production, but above all because in his view 'Brecht was pursuing a chimera':

Brecht said he wanted a kind of music to which lengthy epics can be narrated. After all, Homer was sung. He used to say, 'Isn't it possible to write a setting or note down a cadence that would permit the delivery of a two-hour epic?'

By his own account Eisler made one or two sketches before deciding that this was beyond him. In 1953 therefore when Brecht determined to stage the play himself with the Ensemble he went instead to Paul Dessau, who had already in America been interested enough in the 'Augsburg Chalk Circle' version of the story to draft out the framework of an oratorio. Following very much the requirements posed by Brecht in the note on p. 101, Dessau provided him with the kind of orientally-derived music which he wanted for his recycling of a popular narrative tradition still observable in North Africa and the Far East. According to the composer's *Notizen zu Noten* (Reclam, Leipzig 1947), he made use of Azerbaijani folk-tunes and rounded the play off with an extended dance which Brecht never staged. The production itself took about eight months to rehearse before its première in June 1954. Though it fell foul of the party critics in East Germany it made a great impression at the Paris International Theatre Festival the following year, since when the play has been among the best-known of Brecht's works. After 1964 it was even one of those most performed in the USSR, though according to the critic Kats (reported by Henry Glade), the prologue is simply not playable before a Soviet audience, presumably because it gives too unreal a picture of conditions there.

Particularly among those who disapprove of his decision to settle finally in East Germany, it has become common to contrast Brecht's six years in America with his seven years in East Berlin. And certainly the latter were not productive so far as his original writing went. But his American record is not all that impressive either, at least by the standards which he had set himself in Scandinavia and before that in pre-Nazi Berlin. Of course his initial difficulties did not last for ever, and some of the poems which he wrote from 1942 on show new qualities of concentrated observation which were a genuine gain; nor were they any the less deeply political for being independent of day-to-day party tactics. Though he always remained in some measure dependent on the goodwill of his fellow exiles, he did gradually make his mark among the non-Germans with whom he came in contact, and here his addiction to English literature, whether classical or criminal, must surely have helped. He worked hard and systematically, witness the 'plan for the day' which he drew up on concluding *The Caucasian Chalk Circle* in Santa Monica in 1944:

> get up 7 A.M. newspaper, radio. make coffee in the little copper pot. morning: work. light lunch at twelve. rest with crime story. afternoon: work or pay visits. evening meal at 7 P.M. then visitors. night: half a page of shakespeare or waley's collection of chinese poems. radio. crime story.

But three of the four 'American' plays are to a greater or lesser extent flawed, and the only one which he chose to stage himself when he had the chance was *The Caucasian Chalk Circle,* whose original translation was dug out by us and revised by the Sterns and Auden in 1959 (and subsequently slightly revised again by James Stern in 1984). Despite its awkward combination of two largely unrelated stories (though these had long been married up in the author's mind) and the uncharacteristic sweetness of the heroine, it is a truly epic work, embodying many of Brecht's special ideas, tastes, and talents. In many opinions it is a masterpiece.

It is significant that although this play was commissioned for a Broadway production Brecht himself could attribute its structure to 'a revulsion against the commercialized dramaturgy of Broadway'. For everything else that Brecht wrote in America, apart from his poems, was written for more or less commercial ends; and if he kicked against the commercial spirit it was surely because he knew that he was being conditioned by it. Most obviously this was so of his film stories, which were without exception what he termed 'daily bread and butter work' even though he could hardly help imbuing them with some of his own qualities (whence, no doubt, their ill success). But *Simone Machard* too was written with one eye at least to the film industry; *Schweyk* was to be a Broadway musical, while not only the other two plays but also the adaptation of *Galileo* were written with Broadway productions in view. For the first time in the fourteen years since the success of *The Threepenny Opera*, Brecht was writing exclusively for the commercial stage in its most nakedly competitive form; nor was anything that he is known to have written in America (apart possibly from a short unpublished ballet libretto for Lotte Goslar) performed by the students, musicians, or left-wing amateurs who had helped to shape some of his most original works. He was never particularly good at working for the box-office or respecting other people's conventions, while his natural cussedness made him spoil any chance he might have had of succeeding: witness his wanton (was it unconsciously deliberate?) antagonizing of Leventhal and Luise Rainer. One might almost say that it was his very failures that justify this group of plays.

Why then did he never make contact with any other form of theatre (or cinema) in the United States during those years? Perhaps it was the result of his experiences over the New York production of *The Mother* in 1935 that alienated him so from the American left-wing stage; certainly he seems to have had little use for the ideas of Odets or John Howard Lawson, while even so good a friend as Gorelik was largely in disagreement with him. Nor was university theatre then anything like so active as it has since become. Perhaps too the identification of Hollywood and Broadway with the war effort was itself misleading, for Brecht was always primarily concerned to see the Nazis beaten. *Hangmen, Simone,* and *Schweyk* all deal with the same theme of European resistance to Hitler, while the revised prologue to *The Caucasian Chalk Circle* sets it too within the framework of the war, despite the remoteness of its legend. Oddly enough he never again took up those American themes which had fascinated him earlier, from *In the Jungle of Cities* to *Arturo Ui*, in other words from Munich days right up to his departure from Europe. As Professor James Lyon has pointed out, he did come to take a good deal of interest in the affairs of his half-adopted country and at one point considered basing a script on Edgar Lee Masters's *Spoon River Anthology*; but the only direct reflection of his surroundings is in his poems. Much must have been due to his lack of money and dependence on the German colony's esteem· for him; much too to the lack of his two most-valued women collaborators, Magarete Steffin and Elisabeth Hauptmann (although the latter was then living elsewhere in the US). One can only speculate what might have happened if he had come into contact with the student movement as it later developed, or chosen to associate himself with the blacks. As it was he did not.

He already seems to have decided to return to Germany well before his summons to appear before the House Committee on Un-American Activities in 1947. 1946 is a mysteriously blank year in his life, when he wrote virtually no poems, worked on no plays other than *Galileo*, and made no entries in his journal (unless the relevant pages have somehow been lost). But by that winter he was already planning his return, to judge from his correspondence with Piscator and Caspar Neher, to whom he reported receiving offers 'to be able to use the Theater am Schiffbauerdamm for certain purposes'. His hearing by J. Parnell Thomas's committee the following autumn was in some measure a by-product of their investigation of the motion-picture industry, though his only real link with the so-called Hollywood Ten was his friendship with Donald Ogden Stewart and his wife. What clearly was of more interest to the investigators was his association with Hanns Eisler and through him with his brother Gerhart, the one genuinely important international Communist functionary whom they were able to unearth. This was in some measure due to the Eislers' sister Ruth Fischer, who had been one of the leaders of the German Communist Party in her youth, knew Brecht, and now coined the pleasant phrase for him 'minstrel of the GPU'. Hanns was effectively deported in February 1948; Gerhart (whose prosecution was called for by Richard Nixon in his maiden speech as a Representative) left the US on a Polish liner and was lucky to escape arrest. Brecht stood up well under examination, made the committee laugh, and left for Europe under his own steam a day later. He never came back.

The Editors

The Caucasian Chalk Circle

Collaborator: R. BERLAU

Translators: JAMES AND TANIA STERN, *with* W. H. AUDEN

Characters

Delegates of the Galinsk goat-breeding kolchos: an old peasant, a peasant woman, a young peasant, a very young workman · Members of the Rosa Luxemburg fruit-growing kolchos: an old peasant, a peasant woman, the agronomist, the girl tractor driver; the wounded soldier and other peasants from the kolchos · The expert from the capital · The singer Arkadi Cheidze · His musicians · Georgi Abashvili, the Governor · His wife, Natella · Their son, Michael · Shalva, the adjutant · Arsen Kazbeki, the fat prince · The rider from the capital · Niko Mikadze and Mikha Loladze, doctors · Simon Chachava, a soldier · Grusha Vachnadze, a kitchen-maid · Three architects · Four chambermaids: Assia, Masha, Sulika and Fat Nina · A nurse · A man cook · A woman cook · A stableman · Servants in the governor's palace · The governor's and the fat prince's Ironshirts and soldiers · Beggars and petitioners · The old peasant with the milk · Two elegant ladies · The innkeeper · The servant · A corporal · 'Blockhead', a soldier · A peasant woman and her husband · Three merchants · Lavrenti Vachnadze, Grusha's brother · His wife, Aniko · Their stableman · The peasant woman, for a time Grusha's mother-in-law · Yussup, her son · Brother Anastasius, a monk · Wedding guests · Children · Azdak, the village clerk · Shauva, a policeman · A refugee, the Grand Duke · The doctor · The invalid · The limping man · The blackmailer · Ludovica, the innkeeper's daughter-in-law · A poor old peasant woman · Her brother-in-law Irakli, a bandit · Three farmers · Illo Shaboladze and Sandro Oboladze, lawyers · The very old married couple

THE STRUGGLE FOR THE VALLEY

Among the ruins of a badly shelled Caucasian village the members of two kolchos villages are sitting in a circle, smoking and drinking wine. They consist mainly of women and old men, but there are also a few soldiers among them. With them is an expert of the State Reconstruction Commission from the capital.

A PEASANT WOMAN *left, pointing:* In those hills over there we stopped three Nazi tanks. But the apple orchard had already been destroyed.

AN OLD PEASANT *right:* Our beautiful dairy farm. All in ruins.

A GIRL TRACTOR DRIVER *left:* I set fire to it, Comrade. *Pause.*

THE EXPERT: Now listen to the report: the delegates of the Galinsk goat-breeding kolchos arrived in Nukha. When the Hitler armies were approaching, the kolchos had been ordered by the authorities to move its goat-herds further to the east. The kolchos now considers resettling in this valley. Its delegates have investigated the village and the grounds and found a high degree of destruction. *The delegates on the right nod.* The neighbouring Rosa Luxemburg fruit-growing kolchos—*to the left*—moves that the former grazing land of the Galinsk kolchos, a valley with scanty growth of grass, should be used for the replanting of orchards and vineyards. As an expert of the Reconstruction Commission, I request the two kolchos villages to decide between themselves whether the Galinsk kolchos shall return here or not.

AN OLD MAN *right:* First of all, I want to protest against the restriction of time for discussion. We of the Galinsk kolchos have spent three days and three nights getting here. And now we are allowed a discussion of only half a day.

A WOUNDED SOLDIER *left:* Comrade, we no longer have as many villages and no longer as many working hands and no longer as much time.

THE GIRL TRACTOR DRIVER *left:* All pleasures have to be rationed. Tobacco is rationed, and wine and discussion, too.

THE OLD MAN *right, sighing:* Death to the Fascists! But I will come to the point and explain to you why we want to have our valley back. There are a great many reasons, but I want to begin with one of the simplest. Makinae Abakidze, unpack the goat cheese.

A peasant woman, right, takes from a basket an enormous cheese wrapped in a cloth. Applause and laughter.

Help yourselves, comrades. Start in.

AN OLD PEASANT *left, suspiciously:* Is this meant to influence us, perhaps?

THE OLD MAN *right, amidst laughter:* How could it be meant as an influence, Surab, you valley-thief? Everyone knows that you will take the cheese and the valley, too. *Laughter.* All I expect from you is an honest answer: Do you like the cheese?

THE OLD MAN *left:* The answer is yes.

THE OLD MAN *right:* Oh. *Bitterly.* I might have guessed you know nothing about cheese.

THE OLD MAN *left:* Why not? When I tell you I like it!

THE OLD MAN *right:* Because you can't like it. Because it's not what it was in the old days. And why isn't it? Because our goats don't like the new grass as they used to like the old. Cheese is not cheese because grass is not grass, that's it. Mind you put that in your report.

THE OLD MAN *left:* But your cheese is excellent.

THE OLD MAN *right:* It's not excellent. Barely decent. The new grazing land is no good, whatever the young people may say. I tell you, it's impossible to live there. It doesn't even smell of morning there in the morning.

Several people laugh.

THE EXPERT: Don't mind their laughter. They understand you all the same. Comrades, why does one love one's country? Because the bread tastes better there, the sky is higher, the air smells better, voices sound stronger, the ground is easier to walk on. Isn't that so?

THE OLD MAN *right:* The valley has belonged to us for centuries.

THE SOLDIER *left:* What does that mean—for centuries? Nothing belongs to anyone for centuries. When you were young you didn't even belong to yourself, but to Prince Kazbeki.

THE OLD MAN *right:* According to the law the valley belongs to us.

THE GIRL TRACTOR DRIVER: The laws will have to be re-examined in any case, to see whether they are still valid.

THE OLD MAN *right:* That's obvious. You mean to say it makes no difference what kind of tree stands beside the house where one was born? Or what kind of neighbour one has? Doesn't that make any difference? We want to go back just to have you next door to our kolchos, you valley-thieves. Now you can laugh that one off.

THE OLD MAN *left, laughing:* Then why don't you listen to what your 'neighbour', Kato Vachtang, our agronomist, has to say about the valley?

A PEASANT WOMAN *right:* We haven't said anywhere near all we have to say about our valley. Not all the houses are destroyed. At least the foundation wall of the dairy farm is still standing.

THE EXPERT: You can claim State support—both here and there. You know that.

A PEASANT WOMAN *right:* Comrade Expert, we're not trading now. I can't take your cap and hand you another, and say: 'This one's better.' The other one might be better, but you prefer yours.

THE GIRL TRACTOR DRIVER: A piece of land is not like a cap. Not in our country, comrade.

THE EXPERT: Don't get angry. It's true that we have to consider a piece of land as a tool with which one produces something useful. But it's also true that we must recognize the love for a particular piece of land. Before we continue the discussion I suggest that you explain to the comrades of the Galinsk kolchos just what you intend to do with the disputed valley.

THE OLD MAN *right:* Agreed.

THE OLD MAN *left:* Yes, let Kato speak.

THE EXPERT: Comrade Agronomist!

THE AGRONOMIST *rising. She is in military uniform:* Last winter, comrades, while we were fighting here in these hills as partisans, we discussed how after the expulsion of the Germans we could increase our orchards to ten times their former size. I have prepared a plan for an irrigation project. With the help of a dam on our mountain lake, three hundred hectares of unfertile land can be irrigated. Our kolchos could then grow not only more fruit, but wine as well. The project, however, would pay only if the disputed valley of the Galinsk kolchos could also be included. Here are the calculations. *She hands the expert a briefcase.*

THE OLD MAN *right:* Write into the report that our kolchos plans to start a new stud farm.

THE GIRL TRACTOR DRIVER: Comrades, the project was conceived during the days and nights when we had to take cover in the mountains and often were without ammunition for our few rifles. Even to get a pencil was difficult.

Applause from both sides.

THE OLD MAN *right:* Our thanks to the comrades of the Rosa Luxemburg kolchos and to all those who defended our country.

They shake hands and embrace.

THE PEASANT WOMAN *left:* Our thoughts were that our soldiers—both your men and our men—should return to a still more fertile homeland.

THE GIRL TRACTOR DRIVER: As the poet Mayakovsky said: 'The home of the Soviet people shall also be the home of Reason!'

The delegates on the right (except the old man) have risen and, with the expert, study the agronomist's plans. Exclamations such as: 'Why is there a fall of 66 feet?'—'This rock here is to be dynamited!'—'Actually, all they need is cement and dynamite!'— 'They force the water to come down here, that's clever!'

A VERY YOUNG WORKMAN *right, to the old man, right:* They are going to irrigate all the fields between the hills—look at that, Alleko.

THE OLD MAN *right:* I am not going to look at it. I knew the project would be good. I won't have a revolver pointed at my chest.

THE SOLDIER: But they are only pointing a pencil at your chest.

Laughter.

THE OLD MAN *right. He gets up gloomily and walks over to look at the drawings:* These valley-thieves know only too well that we can't resist machines and projects in this country.

THE PEASANT WOMAN *right:* Alleko Bereshvili, you yourself are the worst one at new projects. That is well known.

THE EXPERT: What about my report? May I write that in your kolchos you will support the transfer of your old valley for the project?

THE PEASANT WOMAN *right:* I will support it. What about you, Alleko?

THE OLD MAN *right, bent over the drawings:* I move that you give us copies of the drawings to take along.

THE PEASANT WOMAN *right:* Then we can sit down to eat. Once he has the drawings and is ready to discuss them, the affair is settled. I know him. And it will be the same with the rest of us.

The delegates embrace again amidst laughter.

THE OLD MAN *left:* Long live the Galinsk kolchos and good luck to your new stud farm!

THE PEASANT WOMAN *left:* Comrades, in honour of the visit of the delegates from the Galinsk kolchos and of the expert we have arranged a play featuring the singer Arkadi Cheidze, which has some bearing on our problem.

Applause.

The girl tractor driver has gone off to fetch the singer.

THE PEASANT WOMAN *right:* Comrades, your play will have to be good. We're going to pay for it with a valley.

THE PEASANT WOMAN *left:* Arkadi Cheidze knows 21,000 verses by heart.

THE OLD MAN *left:* We rehearsed the play under his direction. It is very difficult to get him, by the way. You and the Planning Commission should see to it that he comes north more often, comrade.

THE EXPERT: We are more concerned with economy.

THE OLD MAN *left, smiling:* You arrange the new distribution of grapevines and tractors. Why not of songs, too?

Enter the singer Arkadi Cheidze, led by the girl tractor driver. He is a sturdy man of simple manners, accompanied by musicians with their instruments. The artistes are greeted with applause.

THE GIRL TRACTOR DRIVER: This is the comrade expert, Arkadi.

The singer greets those round him.

THE PEASANT WOMAN *right:* I am very honoured to make your acquaintance. I've heard about your songs ever since I was at school.

THE SINGER: This time it's a play with songs, and almost the whole kolchos takes part. We have brought along the old masks.

THE OLD MAN *right:* Is it going to be one of the old legends?

THE SINGER: A very old one. It is called 'The Chalk Circle' and is derived from the Chinese. But we will recite it in a changed version. Yura, show the masks. Comrades, we consider it an honour to entertain you after such a difficult debate. We hope you will find that the voice of the old poet also sounds well in the shadow of Soviet tractors. It may be mistaken to mix different wines, but old and new wisdom mix very well. Now I hope we will all be given something to eat before the recital begins. That usually helps.

VOICES: Of course.—Everyone into the club house.

All go cheerfully to the meal. While they begin to move off, the expert turns to the singer.

THE EXPERT: How long will the story take, Arkadi? I have to get back to Tiflis tonight.

THE SINGER *casually:* It is actually two stories. A few hours.

THE EXPERT *very confidentially:* Couldn't you make it shorter?

THE SINGER: No.

2

THE NOBLE CHILD   *Scene to the church and the palace*

THE SINGER, *who is seen sitting on the floor in front of his musicians, a black sheepskin cloak round his shoulders, leafing through a small, well-thumbed script:*

> Once upon a time
> A time of bloodshed
> When this city was called
> The city of the damned
> It had a Governor.
> His name was Georgi Abashvili
> Once upon a time.

> He was very rich
> He had a beautiful wife
> He had a healthy child
> Once upon a time.

> No other governor in Grusinia
> Had as many horses in his stable
> As many beggars on his doorstep
> As many soldiers in his service
> As many petitioners in his courtyard
> Once upon a time.

> Georgi Abashvili, how shall I describe him?
> He enjoyed his life:
> On Easter Sunday morning
> The Governor and his family went to church
> Once upon a time.

Beggars and petitioners stream from a palace gateway, holding up thin children, crutches, and petitions. They are followed by two Ironshirts and then by the Governor's family, elaborately dressed.
THE BEGGARS AND PETITIONERS: Mercy, Your Grace, the taxes are beyond our means ... I lost my leg in the

mysterious lighting - like when you tell ghost stories

then the light seems to fade off the singer onto the Gov and procession

Persian War, where can I get . . . My brother is innocent,
Your Grace, a misunderstanding . . . My child is starving
in my arms . . . We plead for our son's discharge from the
army, our one remaining son . . . Please, Your Grace, the
water inspector is corrupt.

*A servant collects the petitions, another distributes coins from a
purse. Soldiers push back the crowd, lashing at it with thick
leather whips.*

SOLDIER: Get back! Make way at the church door!

*Behind the Governor, his wife and his Adjutant, the Governor's
child is driven through the gateway in an ornate pram. The crowd
surges forward to see it.*

THE SINGER *while the crowd is driven back with whips:*

For the first time on this Easter Sunday, the people see
the heir.

Two doctors never leave the child, the noble child

Apple of the Governor's eye.

*Cries from the crowd: 'The child!' . . . 'I can't see it, stop pushing!'
. . . 'God bless the child, Your Grace!'*

THE SINGER:

Even the mighty Prince Kazbeki

Bows before it at the church door.

A fat prince steps forward and bows before the family.

THE FAT PRINCE: Happy Easter, Natella Abashvili!

*A command is heard. A rider arrives at the gallop and holds out to
the Governor a roll of documents. At a nod from the Governor the
Adjutant, a handsome young man, approaches the rider and stops
him. There follows a brief pause during which the fat prince eyes the
rider suspiciously.*

THE FAT PRINCE: What a magnificent day! While it was
raining in the night I thought to myself: gloomy holidays.
But this morning: a gay sky. I love a bright sky, a simple
heart, Natella Abashvili. And little Michael, a governor
from head to foot, tititi! *He tickles the child.* Happy Easter,
little Michael, tititi!

THE GOVERNOR'S WIFE: What do you think of this,
Arsen? Georgi has finally decided to start building the new

wing on the east side. All these miserable slum houses are to be torn down to make room for a garden.

THE FAT PRINCE: That's good news after so much bad. What's the latest about the war, Brother Georgi? *The Governor shows his lack of interest.* A strategic retreat, I hear? Well, minor reverses invariably occur. Sometimes things go well, sometimes not so well. Such are the fortunes of war. Doesn't mean much, eh?

THE GOVERNOR'S WIFE: He's coughing! Georgi, did you hear?

Sharply to the two doctors, dignified men, who stand close to the pram: He's coughing!

FIRST DOCTOR *to the second:* May I remind you, Niko Mikadze, that I was against the lukewarm bath? A minor oversight in warming the bath water, Your Grace.

SECOND DOCTOR *equally polite:* I can't possibly agree with you, Mikha Loladze. The temperature of the bath water was the one prescribed by our great and beloved Mishiko Oboladze. More likely a slight draught in the night, Your Grace.

THE GOVERNOR'S WIFE: But do take better care of him. He looks feverish, Georgi.

FIRST DOCTOR *bending over the child:* No cause for alarm, Your Grace. The bath water will be warmer. It won't happen again.

SECOND DOCTOR *with a poisonous glance at the first:* I won't forget it, dear Mikha Loladze. No cause for alarm, Your Grace.

THE FAT PRINCE: Well, well, well! I always say: one pain in my liver and the doctor gets fifty strokes on the soles of his feet. And that's only because we live in such a decadent age. In the old days it would have been: Off with his head!

THE GOVERNOR'S WIFE: Let's go into the church. Very likely it's the draught here.

The procession, consisting of the family and servants, turns into the church doorway. The fat prince follows. The Adjutant leaves the procession and points at the rider.

THE GOVERNOR: Not before divine service, Shalva.

ADJUTANT *to the rider*: The Governor doesn't want to be bothered with reports before the service—especially if they are, as I suspect, of a depressing nature. Go and get yourself something to eat in the kitchen, my friend.

The Adjutant joins the procession while the rider enters the palace gateway, cursing. A soldier appears from the palace and remains standing in the gateway.

THE SINGER

The city lies still.

On the church square the pigeons preen themselves.

A soldier of the palace guard

Is jesting with the kitchen maid

As she comes up from the river with a bundle.

A girl tries to pass through the gateway, a bundle of large green leaves under her arm.

THE SOLDIER: What! The young lady is not in church? Shirking service?

GRUSHA: I was already dressed to go. But they wanted one more goose for the Easter banquet. And they asked me to fetch it. I know something about geese.

THE SOLDIER: A goose? *Feigning suspicion.* I'd like to see that goose.

Grusha doesn't understand.

One has to be on one's guard with women. They say: 'I only went to fetch a goose', and then it turns out to be something quite different.

GRUSHA *walks resolutely towards him and shows him the goose:* There it is. And if it isn't a fifteen-pound goose, and they haven't stuffed it with corn, I'll eat the feathers.

THE SOLDIER: A queen of a goose. It will be eaten by the Governor himself. So the young lady has been down to the river again?

GRUSHA: Yes, at the poultry farm.

THE SOLDIER: I see! At the poultry farm, down by the river. Not higher up, near those—those willows?

GRUSHA: I go to the willows only to wash linen.

THE SOLDIER *insinuatingly:* Exactly.

GRUSHA: Exactly what?

THE SOLDIER *winking:* Exactly that.

GRUSHA: Why shouldn't I wash my linen near the willows?

THE SOLDIER *with exaggerated laughter:* 'Why shouldn't I wash my linen near the willows!' That's a good one, that is!

GRUSHA: I don't understand the soldier. What's so good about it?

THE SOLDIER *slyly:* If someone knew what someone's told, she'd grow hot, she'd grow cold.

GRUSHA: I don't know what I could know about those willows.

THE SOLDIER: Not even if there were a bush opposite? From which everything could be seen? Everything that happens there when a certain person is washing linen?

GRUSHA: What happens there? Won't the soldier say what he means and have done with it?

THE SOLDIER: Something happens. And perhaps something can be seen.

GRUSHA: Could the soldier mean that—once in a while on a hot day—I put my toes in the water? For otherwise there's nothing.

THE SOLDIER: And more—the toes and more.

GRUSHA: More what? At most the foot.

THE SOLDIER: The foot and a little more. *He laughs heartily.*

GRUSHA *angrily:* Simon Chachava, you ought to be ashamed of yourself! To sit in a bush on a hot day and wait till someone comes along and puts her leg in the river! And most likely with another soldier! *She runs off.*

THE SOLDIER *shouting after her:* Not with another soldier!

As the singer resumes his story the soldier runs after Grusha.

THE SINGER

    The city lies still, but why are there armed men?

    The Governor's palace lies at peace

    But why is it a fortress?

From the doorway at the left the fat prince enters quickly. He stands still and looks around. Before the gateway at the right two Ironshirts are waiting. Noticing them, the prince walks slowly past them, signs to them, then exits quickly. One Ironshirt exits through the gateway, the other remains on guard. Muffled voices come from different sides in the rear: 'To your posts!' The palace is surrounded. Distant church bells. Enter through the doorway the procession and the Governor's family returning from church.

THE SINGER

Then the Governor returned to his palace
Then the fortress was a trap
Then the goose was plucked and roasted
Then the goose was no longer eaten
Then noon was no longer the hour to eat
Then noon was the hour to die.

THE GOVERNOR'S WIFE *in passing:* It's quite impossible to live in this slum. But Georgi, of course, builds only for his little Michael. Never for me. Michael is everything, everything for Michael!

THE GOVERNOR: Did you hear Brother Kazbeki bid me a 'Happy Easter'? That's all very well, but so far as I know it didn't rain in Nukha last night. It rained where Brother Kazbeki was. Where was Brother Kazbeki?

THE ADJUTANT: That will have to be investigated.

THE GOVERNOR: Yes, at once. Tomorrow.

The procession turns into the gateway. The rider, who has meanwhile returned from the palace, walks towards the Governor.

THE ADJUTANT: Don't you want to listen to the rider from the capital, Your Excellency? He arrived this morning with confidential papers.

THE GOVERNOR *in passing:* Not before the banquet, Shalva!

THE ADJUTANT *to the rider, while the procession disappears into the palace and only two Ironshirts remain at the gate as palace guards:* The Governor doesn't wish to be disturbed by military reports before the banquet. The afternoon His Excellency will devote to conferences with prominent architects who have also been invited to the banquet. Here they are already. *Enter three men. As the rider goes off, the Adjutant greets the architects.* Gentlemen, His Excellency is awaiting you at the banquet. His entire time will be devoted to you. To the great new plans! Come, let us go!

ONE OF THE ARCHITECTS: We are impressed that his Excellency thinks of building in spite of the disquieting rumours that the war in Persia has taken a turn for the worse.

THE ADJUTANT: All the more reason for building! That's nothing. Persia is far away. The garrison here would let itself be chopped to pieces for its Governor. *Uproar from the palace. Shrill screams of a woman. Orders are shouted. Dumbfounded, the Adjutant moves towards the gateway. An Ironshirt steps out and holds him up at the point of a lance.* What's going on here? Put down that lance, you dog! *To the palace guard, furiously.* Disarm him! Can't you see an attempt is being made on the Governor's life? *The palace guard Ironshirts refuse to obey. Staring coldly, indifferently, at the Adjutant, they watch the proceedings without interest. The Adjutant fights his way into the palace.*

ONE OF THE ARCHITECTS: The Princes! Don't you realize that the Princes met last night in the capital? And that they are against the Grand Duke and his governors? Gentlemen, we'd better make ourselves scarce. *They rush off.*

THE SINGER

Oh, blindness of the great! They walk like gods
Great over bent backs, sure
Of hired fists, trusting
In their power which has already lasted so long.
But long is not forever.
Oh, Wheel of Fortune! Hope of the people!

From the gateway, enter the Governor with a grey face, manacled, between two soldiers armed to the teeth.

Walk, Your Highness, walk even now with head up.
From your Palace the eyes of many foes follow you!
You no longer need an architect, a carpenter will do.

You will not move into a new palace, but into a little hole
in the ground.
Just look about you once more, you blind man!
The arrested Governor looks about him.
Does all you once possessed still please you? Between the
Easter Mass and the banquet
You are walking to that place from which no one returns.
*The Governor is led away. The palace guard follows. A horn
sounds. Noise behind the gateway.*
When the houses of the great collapse
Many little people are slain.
Those who had no share in the fortunes of the mighty
Often have a share in their misfortunes. The plunging
wain
Drags the sweating beasts with it into the abyss.
Servants come rushing through the gateway in panic.
THE SERVANTS *in confusion:* The hampers!—Take them all
into the third courtyard! Food for five days!—Her Ladyship has fainted! Someone must carry her down. She must
get away.—And what about us? We'll be slaughtered like
chickens, it's the old story.—Jesus and Mary, what's going
to happen? There's already bloodshed in the town, they
say.—Nonsense, the Governor has just been asked politely
to appear at a Princes' meeting. Everything'll be all right. I
have this on the best authority.
The two doctors rush into the courtyard.
FIRST DOCTOR *trying to restrain the other:* Niko Mikadze, it is
your duty as a doctor to attend Natella Abashvili.
SECOND DOCTOR: My duty? It's yours!
FIRST DOCTOR: Niko Mikadze, who is in charge of the child
today? You or me?
SECOND DOCTOR: Do you really think, Mikha Loladze, I'm
going to stay another minute in this cursed house for that
little brat?
*They start fighting. All one hears is: 'You neglect your duty!' and
'Duty be damned!' Then the second doctor knocks down the first.*
SECOND DOCTOR: Oh, go to hell! *Exit.*

THE SERVANTS: There's time enough before night. The soldiers won't be drunk till then.—Does anyone know if they've started a mutiny yet?—The Palace Guard has ridden away.—Doesn't anyone know what's happened?

GRUSHA: Meliva the fisherman says a comet with a red tail has been seen in the sky over the capital. That means bad luck.

THE SERVANTS: Yesterday they were saying in the capital that the Persian War is lost.—The Princes have started a great revolt. There's a rumour that the Grand Duke has already fled. All his Governors are to be hanged.—The likes of us will be left alone. I have a brother in the Ironshirts.

Enter the soldier Simon Chachava, searching the crowd for Grusha.

THE ADJUTANT *appearing in the doorway:* Everyone into the third courtyard! All hands help with the packing!

He drives the servants out. Simon finally finds Grusha.

SIMON: There you are at last, Grusha! What are you going to do?

GRUSHA: Nothing. If the worst comes to the worst, I've a brother with a farm in the mountains. But what about you?

SIMON: Don't worry about me. *Polite again.* Grusha Vachnadze, your desire to know my plans fills me with satisfaction. I've been ordered to accompany Madam Natella Abashvili as her guard.

GRUSHA: But hasn't the Palace Guard mutinied?

SIMON *serious:* That they have.

GRUSHA: But isn't it dangerous to accompany the woman?

SIMON: In Tiflis they say: how can stabbing harm the knife?

GRUSHA: You're not a knife. You're a man, Simon Chachava. What has this woman to do with you?

SIMON: The woman has nothing to do with me. But I have my orders, and so I go.

GRUSHA: The soldier is a pig-headed man; he gets himself into danger for nothing—nothing at all. *As she is called from the palace:* Now I must go into the third courtyard. I'm in a hurry.

SIMON: As there's a hurry we oughtn't to quarrel. For a good quarrel one needs time. May I ask if the young lady still has parents?

GRUSHA: No, only a brother.

SIMON: As time is short—the second question would be: Is the young lady as healthy as a fish in water?

GRUSHA: Perhaps once in a while a pain in the right shoulder; but otherwise strong enough for any work. So far no one has complained.

SIMON: Everyone knows that. Even if it's Easter Sunday and there's the question who shall fetch the goose, then it's she. The third question is this: Is the young lady impatient? Does she want cherries in winter?

GRUSHA: Impatient, no. But if a man goes to war without any reason, and no message comes, that's bad.

SIMON: A message will come. *Grusha is again called from the palace.* And finally the main question . . .

GRUSHA: Simon Chachava, because I've got to go to the third courtyard and I'm in a hurry, the answer is 'Yes'.

SIMON *very embarrassed:* Hurry, they say, is the wind that blows down the scaffolding. But they also say: The rich don't know what hurry is.—I come from . . .

GRUSHA: Kutsk.

SIMON: So the young lady has already made inquiries? Am healthy, have no dependents, earn ten piastres a month, as a paymaster twenty, and am asking honourably for your hand.

GRUSHA: Simon Chachava, that suits me.

SIMON *taking from his neck a thin chain from which hangs a little cross:* This cross belonged to my mother, Grusha Vach-nadze. The chain is silver. Please wear it.

GRUSHA: I thank you, Simon. *He fastens it round her neck.*

SIMON: Now I must harness the horses. The young lady will understand that. It would be better for the young lady to go into the third courtyard. Otherwise there'll be trouble.

GRUSHA: Yes, Simon.

They stand together undecided.

SIMON: I'll just take the woman to the troops who've remained loyal. When the war's over, I'll come back. In two weeks. Or three. I hope my intended won't get tired waiting for my return.

GRUSHA: Simon Chachava, I shall wait for you.

> Go calmly into battle, soldier
> The bloody battle, the bitter battle
> From which not everyone returns.
> When you return I will be there.
> I will be waiting for you under the green elm
> I will be waiting for you under the bare elm
> I will wait until the last soldier has returned
> And even longer.
> When you return from the battle
> No boots will lie before the door
> The pillow beside mine will be empty
> My mouth will be unkissed.
> When you return, when you return
> You will be able to say: all is as it was.

SIMON: I thank you, Grusha Vachnadze, and farewell!
He bows low before her; she bows low before him. Then she runs off without looking round. Enter the Adjutant from the gateway.

THE ADJUTANT *harshly:* Harness the horses to the big carriage! Don't stand there doing nothing, idiot!
Simon Chachava leaps to attention and goes off. Two servants crawl in from the gateway, loaded down with heavy trunks. Behind them, supported by her women, stumbles Natella Abashvili. She is followed by another woman carrying Michael.

THE GOVERNOR'S WIFE: As usual, nobody's paying the slightest attention. I hardly know if I'm standing on my head or my feet. Where's Michael? Don't hold him so clumsily! Pile the trunks on to the carriage! Shalva, is there any word from the Governor?

THE ADJUTANT *shaking his head:* You must get away at once.

THE GOVERNOR'S WIFE: Is there any news from the town?

Trunks w/ clothing to throw around

THE ADJUTANT: No. So far all is quiet. But there isn't a minute to lose. There's not enough room for the trunks on the carriage. Please pick out what you need.

Exit the Adjutant quickly.

THE GOVERNOR'S WIFE: Only essentials! Quick, open the trunks. I'll tell you what I've got to have.

The trunks are lowered and opened.

THE GOVERNOR'S WIFE *pointing at some brocade dresses:* That green one! And of course that one with the fur trimming. Where are the doctors? I'm getting this terrible migraine again. It always starts in the temples. This one with the little pearl buttons . . . *Enter Grusha.* You're taking your time, eh? Go and get the hot water bottles at once!

Grusha runs off, and returns with hot water bottles. The Governor's wife orders her about by signs.

THE GOVERNOR'S WIFE *watching a young woman attendant:* Don't tear the sleeve!

THE YOUNG WOMAN: I promise you, madam, no harm has come to the dress.

THE GOVERNOR'S WIFE: Because I caught you. I've been watching you for a long time. Nothing in your head but making eyes at the Adjutant. I'll kill you, you bitch! *She beats her.*

THE ADJUTANT *returning:* I must ask you to make haste, Natella Abashvili. They are fighting in the town. *Exit the Adjutant.*

THE GOVERNOR'S WIFE *letting go of the young woman:* My God, do you think they'll do something to me? Why should they? *All are silent. She herself begins to rummage in the trunks.* Where's my brocade jacket? Help me! What about Michael? Is he asleep?

THE NURSE: Yes, madam.

THE GOVERNOR'S WIFE: Then put him down a moment and go and fetch my little morocco slippers from the bedchamber. I need them to go with the green dress. *The nurse puts down the child and goes off. To the young woman:* Don't stand around, you! *The young woman runs off.* Stay here, or I'll have you flogged! Just look at the way these things have been packed! No love! No understanding! If one doesn't give every order oneself . . . At such moments one realizes what one's servants are like! Masha! *She gives her an order with a wave of the hand.* You all gorge yourselves, but never a sign of gratitude! I won't forget this.

THE ADJUTANT *very excited:* Natella, you must leave at once! Orbeliani, Judge of the Supreme Court, has just been hanged! The carpet weavers are in revolt!

THE GOVERNOR'S WIFE: Why? I must have the silver dress —it cost 1000 piastres. And that one there, and all my furs. And where's the wine-coloured dress?

THE ADJUTANT *trying to pull her away:* Riots have broken out in the outer town! We've got to leave this minute! *A servant runs off.* Where's the child?

THE GOVERNOR'S WIFE *to the nurse:* Maro, get the child ready! Where are you?

THE ADJUTANT *leaving:* We'll probably have to do without the carriage. And ride.

The Governor's wife still rummages among her dresses, throws some on to the heap to go with her, then takes them off again. Drums are heard. The sky begins to redden.

THE GOVERNOR'S WIFE *rummaging desperately:* I can't find that wine-coloured dress. *Shrugging her shoulders, to the second woman:* Take the whole heap and carry it to the carriage. Why hasn't Maro come back? Have you all gone off your heads? I told you it's right at the bottom.

THE ADJUTANT *returning:* Quick! Quick!

THE GOVERNOR'S WIFE *to the second woman:* Run! Just throw them into the carriage!

THE ADJUTANT: We're not going by carriage. Come at once or I'll ride off on my own!

THE GOVERNOR'S WIFE: Maro! Bring the child! *To the second woman:* Go and look, Masha. No, first take the dresses to the carriage. It's all nonsense, I wouldn't dream of riding! *Turning round, she sees the fire-reddened sky and starts back in horror.* Fire! *She rushes off, followed by the Adjutant. The second woman, shaking her head, follows with a heap of dresses. Servants enter from the gateway.*

THE COOK: That must be the East Gate that's burning.

THE CHEF: They've gone. And without the food wagon. How are we going to get away now?

A STABLEMAN: This is going to be an unhealthy place for some time. *To the third chambermaid:* Suleika, I'm going to fetch some blankets, we're clearing out.

THE NURSE *entering through the gateway with her mistress's slippers:* Madam!

A FAT WOMAN: She's gone.

THE NURSE: And the child. *She rushes to the child, and picks it up.* They left it behind, those brutes! *She hands the child to Grusha.* Hold it for a moment. *Deceitfully.* I'm going to look for the carriage.

She runs off, following the Governor's wife.

GRUSHA: What have they done to the Governor?

THE STABLEMAN *drawing his index finger across his throat:* Fft.

THE FAT WOMAN *seeing the gesture, becomes hysterical:* Oh God! Oh God! Oh God! Our master Georgi Abashvili! At morning Mass he was a picture of health! And now! Oh, take me away! We're all lost! We must die in sin! Like our master, Georgi Abashvili!

THE THIRD WOMAN *trying to calm her:* Calm down, Nina. You'll get away. You've done no one any harm.

THE FAT WOMAN *being led out:* Oh God! Oh God! Oh God! Let's all get out before they come! Before they come!

THE THIRD WOMAN: Nina takes it to heart more than the mistress. People like that get others even to do their weeping for them! *Seeing the child in Grusha's arms.* The child! What are you doing with it?

GRUSHA: It's been left behind.

THE THIRD WOMAN: She just left it? Michael, who was never allowed to be in a draught!

The servants gather round the child.

GRUSHA: He's waking up.

THE STABLEMAN: Better put him down, I tell you. I'd rather not think what'd happen to the person seen with that child. I'll get our things. You wait here. *Exit into the palace.*

THE COOK: He's right. Once they start they slaughter whole families. I'll go and fetch my belongings.

All go except the cook, the third woman and Grusha with the child in her arms.

THE THIRD WOMAN: Didn't you hear? Better put him down!

GRUSHA: The nurse asked me to hold him for a moment.

THE COOK: That one won't come back, you silly!

THE THIRD WOMAN: Keep your hands off him.

THE COOK: They'll be more after him than after his mother. He's the heir. Grusha, you're a good soul. But you know you're not too bright. I tell you, if he had the plague it couldn't be worse. Better see to it that you get away.

The stableman has come back carrying bundles which he distributes among the women. All except Grusha prepare to leave.

GRUSHA *stubbornly:* He hasn't got the plague. He looks at you like a human being.

THE COOK: Then don't you look back. You're just the kind of fool who always gets put upon. If someone says to you: Run and get the lettuce, you have the longest legs!—you run. We're taking the ox-cart, you can have a lift if you hurry. Jesus, by now the whole neighbourhood must be in flames!

THE THIRD WOMAN: Haven't you packed anything yet? There isn't much time, you know. The Ironshirts will soon be here from the barracks.

Exit both women and the stableman.

GRUSHA: I'm coming.

Grusha lays the child down, looks at it for a moment, then takes clothes from the trunks lying about and covers the sleeping child. Then she runs into the palace to get her things. Sounds of horses' hoofs and of women screaming. Enter the fat prince with drunken Ironshirts. One of them carries the head of the Governor on a lance.

THE FAT PRINCE: Put it here. Right in the middle! *One Iron-shirt climbs on to the back of another, takes the head and holds it over the gateway.* That's not the middle. Further to the right. Good. What I do, my friends, I do well. *While an Ironshirt with hammer and nail fastens the head by its hair:* This morning at the church door I said to Georgi Abashvili: 'I love a clear sky'. Actually, what I prefer is lightning from a clear sky. Oh, yes. But it's a pity they took the brat away. I need him. Badly. Search the whole of Grusinia for him! 1000 piastres reward!

As Grusha enters cautiously through the doorway, the fat prince and the Ironshirts leave. Trampling of horses' hoofs again. Carrying a bundle, Grusha walks towards the gateway. At the last moment, she turns to see if the child is still there. Promptly the singer begins to sing. She stands rooted to the spot.

THE SINGER

As she was standing between courtyard and gate, she
     heard
Or thought she heard, a low voice. The child
Called to her, not whining but calling quite sensibly
At least so it seemed to her: 'Woman', it said, 'Help me'.
Went on calling not whining but calling quite sensibly:
'Don't you know, woman, that she who does not listen to
     a cry for help
But passes by shutting her ears, will never hear
The gentle call of a lover
Nor the blackbird at dawn, nor the happy
Sigh of the exhausted grape-picker at the sound of the
     Angelus.'
Hearing this
Grusha walks a few steps towards the child and bends over it.
          she went back to the child
Just for one more look, just to sit with it
For a moment or two till someone should come
Its mother, perhaps, or someone else—
She sits down opposite the child, and leans against a trunk.
Just for a moment before she left, for now the danger was
     too great
The city full of flame and grief.

The light grows dimmer as though evening and night were falling,
Grusha has gone into the palace and fetched a lamp and some milk,
which she gives the child to drink.

THE SINGER *loudly:*

Terrible is the temptation to do good!

Grusha now settles down to keep watch over the child through the
night. Once, she lights a small lamp to look at it. Once, she tucks it
in with a brocade coat. Now and again she listens and looks up to
see if someone is coming.

For a long time she sat with the child.
Evening came, night came, dawn came.
Too long she sat, too long she watched
The soft breathing, the little fists
Till towards morning the temptation grew too strong.
She rose, she leaned over, she sighed, she lifted the child
She carried it off.
She does what the singer says as he describes it.
Like booty she took it for herself
Like a thief she sneaked away.

3

THE FLIGHT INTO THE NORTHERN MOUNTAINS

THE SINGER

As Grusha Vachnadze left the city
On the Grusinian highway
Towards the northern mountains
She sang a song, she bought some milk.

THE MUSICIANS

How will the merciful escape the merciless
The bloodhounds, the trappers?
Into the deserted mountains she wandered
Along the Grusinian highway she wandered
She sang a song, she bought some milk.

Grusha Vachnadze continues on her way. On her back she carries
the child in a sack, in one hand a bundle, in the other a big stick.

GRUSHA *singing:*

> Four generals set off for Iran
> Four generals but not one man.
> The first did not strike a blow
> The second did not beat the foe
> For the third the weather was not right
> For the fourth the soldiers would not fight.
> Four generals went forth to attack
> Four generals turned back.

> Sosso Robakidse marched to Iran
> Sosso Robakidse was a man.
> He struck a sturdy blow
> He certainly beat the foe
> For him the weather was good enough
> For him the soldiers fought with love
> Sosso Robakidse marched to Iran
> Sosso Robakidse is our man.

A peasant's cottage appears.

GRUSHA *to the child:* Noontime, eating time. Now we'll sit here quietly in the grass, while the good Grusha goes and buys a little jug of milk. *She lays the child down and knocks at the cottage door. An old peasant opens it.* Grandpa, could I have a little mug of milk? And perhaps a corn cake?

THE OLD MAN: Milk? We haven't any milk. The soldiers from the city took our goats. If you want milk, go to the soldiers.

GRUSHA: But Grandpa, you surely have a jug of milk for a child?

THE OLD MAN: And for a 'God Bless You', eh?

GRUSHA: Who said anything about a 'God Bless You'? *She pulls out her purse.* We're going to pay like princes. Head in the clouds, bottom in the water! *The peasant goes off grumbling to fetch milk.* And how much is this jug?

THE OLD MAN: Three piastres. Milk has gone up.

GRUSHA: Three piastres for that drop? *Without a word the old man slams the door in her face.* Michael, did you hear that?

Three piastres! We can't afford that. *She goes back, sits down again and gives the child her breast.* Well, we must try again like this. Suck. Think of the three piastres. There's nothing there, but you think you're drinking, and that's something. *Shaking her head, she realizes the child has stopped sucking. She gets up, walks back to the door, and knocks again.* Open, Grandpa, we'll pay. *Under her breath:* May God strike you! *When the old man appears again:* I thought it would be half a piastre. But the child must have something. What about one piastre?

THE OLD MAN: Two.

GRUSHA: Don't slam the door again. *She rummages a long time in her purse.* Here are two piastres. But this milk has got to last. We still have a long journey ahead of us. These are cutthroat prices. It's a sin.

THE OLD MAN: If you want milk, kill the soldiers.

GRUSHA *letting the child drink:* That's an expensive joke. Drink, Michael. This is half a week's pay. The people here think we've earned our money sitting on our bottom. Michael, Michael, I certainly took on a nice burden with you! *Looking at the brocade coat in which the child is wrapped:* A brocade coat worth 1000 piastres, and not one piastre for milk. *She glances round.* Look! There's a carriage, with rich ladies. We ought to get on to that.

In front of a caravansary. Grusha dressed in the brocade coat is seen approaching two elegant ladies. She holds the child in her arms.

GRUSHA: Oh, you ladies want to spend the night here, too? It's awful how crowded it is everywhere! And not a carriage to be found! My coachman simply turned back. I've been walking half a mile on foot. Barefoot, too! My Persian shoes—you know those heels! But why doesn't someone come?

THE ELDER LADY: That innkeeper certainly takes his time. The whole country has lost its manners since those goings-on started in the capital.

The innkeeper appears, a very dignified old man with a long beard, followed by his servant.

THE INNKEEPER: Excuse an old man for keeping you waiting, ladies. My little grandchild was showing me a peach tree in blossom. There on the slope, beyond the cornfields. We're planting fruit trees there, a few cherries. Further west—*pointing*—the ground gets more stony. That's where the farmers graze their sheep. You ought to see the peach blossom, the pink is exquisite.

THE ELDER LADY: You live in a fertile region.

THE INNKEEPER: God has blessed it. How far on is the fruit-blossom further south, my ladies? I take it you come from the south?

THE YOUNGER LADY: I must admit I haven't been paying much attention to the landscape.

THE INNKEEPER *politely:* Of course, the dust. It is advisable to travel slowly on our high roads. Provided, of course, one isn't in too great a hurry.

THE ELDER LADY: Put your scarf round your throat, dearest. The evening breeze seems rather cool here.

THE INNKEEPER: It comes down from the Janga-Tau glaciers, my ladies.

GRUSHA: Yes, I'm afraid my son may catch cold.

THE ELDER LADY: A very spacious caravansary! Shall we go in?

THE INNKEEPER: Oh, the ladies want rooms? But the caravansary is full up, my ladies. And the servants have run off. I very much regret it, but I cannot accommodate another person, not even with references . . .

THE YOUNGER LADY: But we can't spend the night here on the road.

THE ELDER LADY *drily:* How much?

THE INNKEEPER: My ladies, you will understand that in these times, when so many fugitives, no doubt quite respectable people but not popular with the authorities, are looking for shelter, a house has to be particularly careful. Therefore . . .

THE ELDER LADY: My dear man, we aren't fugitives. We're simply moving to our summer residence in the mountains, that's all. It would never occur to us to ask for hospitality if—we needed it all that urgently.

THE INNKEEPER *nodding his head in agreement:* Of course not. I only doubt if the tiny room at my disposal would suit the ladies. I have to charge 60 piastres per person. Are the ladies together?

GRUSHA: In a way. I'm also in need of shelter.

THE YOUNGER LADY: 60 piastres! That's a cut-throat price.

THE INNKEEPER *coldly:* My ladies, I have no desire to cut throats. That's why . . . *He turns to go.*

THE ELDER LADY: Must we talk about throats? Let's go in. *She enters, followed by the servant.*

THE YOUNGER LADY *desperate:* 180 piastres for one room! *Glancing back at Grusha:* But with the child it's impossible! What if it cries?

THE INNKEEPER: The room costs 180, whether it's two persons or three.

THE YOUNGER LADY *changing her attitude to Grusha:* On the other hand, I couldn't bear to think of you on the road, my dear. Do come in.

They enter the caravansary. From the rear on the opposite side of the stage the servant appears with some luggage. Behind him come the elder lady, the younger lady and Grusha with the child.

THE YOUNGER LADY: 180 piastres! I haven't been so upset since they brought dear Igor home.

THE ELDER LADY: Must you talk about Igor?

THE YOUNGER LADY: Actually, we are four persons. The child is one too, isn't it? *To Grusha:* Couldn't you pay half at least?

GRUSHA: That's impossible. I had to leave in a hurry, you see. And the Adjutant forgot to slip me enough money.

THE ELDER LADY: Perhaps you haven't even got the 60?

GRUSHA: That much I'll pay.

THE YOUNGER LADY: Where are the beds?

THE SERVANT: There aren't any beds. Here are some sacks and blankets. You'll have to arrange them yourselves. Be glad you're not being put in a hole in the earth. Like lots of others. *Exit.*

THE YOUNGER LADY: Did you hear that? I'm going straight to the innkeeper. That man must be flogged.

THE ELDER LADY: Like your husband?

THE YOUNGER LADY: Don't be so cruel! *She weeps.*

THE ELDER LADY: How are we going to arrange something to sleep on?

GRUSHA: I'll see to that. *She puts down the child.* It's always easier when there are several hands. You still have the carriage. *Sweeping the floor.* I was taken completely by surprise. 'My dear Anastasia Katarinovska,' my husband was saying before luncheon, 'do go and lie down for a while. You know how easily you get your migraine.' *She spreads out sacks and makes beds. The ladies, watching her work, exchange glances.* 'Georgi', said I to the Governor, 'I can't lie down when there are sixty for luncheon. And one can't trust the servants. And Michael Georgivich won't eat without me.' *To Michael*: See, Michael? Everything'll be all right, what did I tell you! *She suddenly realizes that the ladies are watching her strangely and whispering.* Well, there we are! At least one doesn't have to lie on the bare floor. I've folded the blankets double.

THE ELDER LADY *imperiously*: You seem to be rather clever at making beds, my dear. Let's have a look at your hands!

GRUSHA *frightened*: What?

THE YOUNGER LADY: You're being asked to show your hands.

Grusha shows the ladies her hands.

THE YOUNGER LADY *triumphant*: Cracked! A servant!

THE ELDER LADY *goes to the door and shouts*: Service!

THE YOUNGER LADY: You're caught! You swindler! Just confess what mischief you're up to!

GRUSHA *confused*: I'm not up to any mischief. I just thought you might take us a little way in your carriage. Please, I ask you, don't make a noise, I'll go on my own.

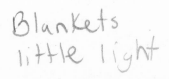
Blankets
little light

THE YOUNGER LADY *while the elder lady continues shouting for service:* Yes, you'll go all right, but with the police. For the moment you'll stay. Don't you dare move, you!

GRUSHA: But I was ready to pay the 60 piastres. Here. *She shows her purse.* Look for yourself. I have them. Here are four tens, and here's a five—no, that's another ten, and ten, makes 60. All I want is to get the child on to the carriage. That's the truth.

THE YOUNGER LADY: Aha, so that's what you want. On to the carriage! Now it's come out.

GRUSHA: Madam, I confess, I am from a humble family. Please don't call the police. The child is of noble birth, look at the linen. It's fleeing, like yourself.

THE YOUNGER LADY: Of noble birth! We know that one. The father's a prince, eh?

GRUSHA *to the elder lady, fiercely:* Stop shouting! Have you no heart at all?

THE YOUNGER LADY *to the elder lady:* Look out! She'll attack you! She's dangerous! Help! Murder!

THE SERVANT *entering:* What's going on here?

THE ELDER LADY: This person here has smuggled herself in by playing the lady. She's probably a thief.

THE YOUNGER LADY: And a dangerous one, too. She wanted to murder us. It's a case for the police. Oh God, I can feel my migraine coming on!

THE SERVANT: There aren't any police at the moment. *To Grusha:* Pack up your things, sister, and make yourself scarce.

GRUSHA *angrily picking up the child:* You monsters! And they're already nailing your heads to the wall!

THE SERVANT *pushing her out:* Shut your trap. Or you'll have the Old Man here. And there's no trifling with him.

THE ELDER LADY *to the younger lady:* Just see if she hasn't stolen something already!

While the ladies, right, look feverishly to see whether something has been stolen, the servant and Grusha go out through the door, left.

THE SERVANT: Look before you leap, I say. Another time have a good look at people before you get mixed up with them.

GRUSHA: I thought they'd be more likely to treat their own kind better.

THE SERVANT: Not them! Believe me, nothing's harder than aping a lazy useless person. Once they suspect you can wipe your own arse, or that your hands have ever touched a broom, the game's up. Just wait a minute, I'll get you a corn cake and a few apples.

GRUSHA: Better not. I must get out before the Old Man comes. And if I walk all night I'll be out of danger, I think. *She walks away.*

THE SERVANT *calling after her in a low voice:* At the next crossroads, turn right. *She disappears.*

THE SINGER:
As Grusha Vachnadze wandered northwards
She was followed by the Prince's Ironshirts.

THE MUSICIANS
How will the barefooted girl escape the Ironshirts
The bloodhounds, the trappers?
They are hunting even by night.
Pursuers don't get tired.
Butchers sleep little.

Two Ironshirts are trudging along the highway.

THE CORPORAL: Blockhead, you'll never amount to anything. Why? Because your heart's not in it. Your superior sees it in little things. Yesterday when I laid that fat woman, I admit you collared her husband as I commanded. And you did kick him in the stomach. But did you enjoy it like a good soldier? Or did you just do it from a sense of duty? I've kept my eyes on you, blockhead. You're like a hollow reed or a tinkling cymbal. You'll never get promoted. *They walk awhile in silence.* Don't you get the idea I don't notice how insubordinate you are in every way. I forbid you to limp! You do it simply because I sold the horses, and I

sold them because I'd never have got that price again.
I know you: you limp just to show me you don't like
marching. But that won't help you. It'll go against you.
Sing!

THE TWO IRONSHIRTS *singing*:

O sadly one morning, one morning in May
I kissed my darling and rode far away.
Protect her, dear friends, until home from the wars
I come riding in triumph, alive on my horse.

THE CORPORAL: Louder!

THE TWO IRONSHIRTS:

When I lie in my grave and my sword turns to rust
My darling shall bring me a handful of dust.
For the feet that so gaily ran up to her door
And the arms that went round her shall please her no
   more.

They begin to walk again in silence.

THE CORPORAL: A good soldier has his heart and soul in it.
He lets himself be hacked to pieces by his superiors, and
even while dying he's aware of his Corporal nodding ap-
proval. For him that's reward enough. That's all he wants.
But *you* won't get a nod. And you'll croak just the same.
Christ, how am I to lay my hands on the Governor's
bastard with an ass like you!

They trudge on.

THE SINGER

When Grusha Vachnadze came to the River Sirra
The flight grew too much for her, the helpless child too
   heavy.

THE MUSICIANS

The rosy dawn in the cornfields
Is nothing but cold to the sleepless.
The gay clatter of the milk cans in the farmyard
Where the smoke rises is nothing but a threat to the
   fugitives.
She who drags the child feels nothing but its weight.

Grusha stops in front of a farm.

GRUSHA: Now you've wetted yourself again, and you know I've no nappies. Michael, we've got to part. This is far enough from the city. They won't want you so badly, little squit, that they'll follow you all this way. The woman looks kind, and just you smell the milk! So farewell, little Michael. I'll forget how you kicked me in the back all night to make me go faster. And you—you forget the meagre fare. It was meant well. I'd love to have kept you, because your nose is so small, but it can't be done. I'd have shown you your first rabbit and—how not to wet yourself, but I must turn back, because my sweetheart the soldier might soon return, and suppose he didn't find me? You can't ask that of me, Michael.

A fat peasant woman carries a milk can to the door. Grusha waits until she has gone in, then gingerly approaches the house. She tiptoes to the door and lays the child on the threshold. Then, hiding behind a tree, she waits until the peasant woman opens the door and sees the bundle.

THE PEASANT WOMAN: Jesus Christ, what's this? Husband!

THE PEASANT: What's up? Let me have my soup.

THE PEASANT WOMAN *to the child:* Where's your mother? Haven't you got one? It's a boy. And the linen is fine; it's from a good family. And they just leave him on our doorstep. Oh, what times we live in!

THE PEASANT: If they think we're going to feed it, they're mistaken. You take it to the priest in the village. That's all we can do.

THE PEASANT WOMAN: What will the priest do with it? It needs a mother. There, it's waking up. Don't you think we could keep it?

THE PEASANT *shouting:* No!

THE PEASANT WOMAN: I could lay it in the corner, next to the armchair. I only need a crib for it. And I can take it into the fields with me. Look how it's smiling! Husband, we have a roof over our heads and we can do it. I won't hear another word.

She carries the child into the house. The peasant follows, protesting.

Grusha steps out from behind the tree, laughs, and hurries away in the opposite direction.

THE SINGER
  Why so gay, you, making for home?
THE MUSICIANS
  Because with a smile the child
  Has won new parents for himself, that's why I'm gay.
  Because I am rid of the loved one
  That's why I'm happy.
THE SINGER
  And why are you sad?
THE MUSICIANS
  I'm sad because I'm single and free
  Of the little burden in whom a heart was beating:
  Like one robbed, like one impoverished I'm going.

Grusha walks for a short while, then meets the two Ironshirts, who hold her up at the point of a lance.

THE CORPORAL: Young lady, you're running into the Armed Forces. Where are you coming from? When are you coming? Are you entertaining illegal relations with the enemy? Where is he hiding? What sort of movements is he making in your rear? What about the hills? What about the valley? How are your stockings fastened?

Grusha stands there frightened.

GRUSHA: They are strongly fastened; you'd better withdraw.
THE CORPORAL: I always withdraw. In that respect I'm reliable. Why are you staring like that at the lance? In the field a soldier never loses control of his lance. That's an order. Learn it by heart, blockhead. Now then, young lady, where are you off to?
GRUSHA: To my intended, one Simon Chachava, of the Palace Guard in Nukha. Wait till I write to him; he'll break your bones for you.
THE CORPORAL: Simon Chachava? Indeed! I know him. He gave me the key so I could keep an eye on you once in a while. Blockhead, we're getting unpopular. We must make her realize we have honourable intentions. Young lady, my

apparent flippancy hides a serious nature. So I'll tell you officially: I want a child from you.

Grusha utters a little scream.

Blockhead, she has understood. Ooh, isn't that a sweet fright! 'But first I must take the bread out of the oven, Officer! But first I must change my torn chemise, Colonel!' But joking apart. Listen, young lady, we are looking for a certain child in these parts. Have you heard of a child from the city, of good family, dressed in fine linen?

GRUSHA: No. I've heard nothing.

THE SINGER

Run, kind heart! The killers are coming!
Help the helpless child, helpless girl! And so she runs.

Suddenly, panic-stricken, she turns round and runs. The Ironshirts glance at each other, then follow her, cursing.

THE MUSICIANS

In the bloodiest times
There are still good people.

As Grusha enters the cottage, the peasant woman is bending over the child's crib.

GRUSHA: Hide it! Quick! The Ironshirts are coming! It was I who laid it on your doorstep. But it isn't mine. It's of a noble family.

THE PEASANT WOMAN: Who's coming? What sort of Ironshirts?

GRUSHA: Don't ask questions. The Ironshirts who are looking for it.

THE PEASANT WOMAN: They've no business in my house. But it seems I must have a word with you.

GRUSHA: Take off the fine linen. That will give us away.

THE PEASANT WOMAN: Oh, you and your linen! In this house *I* decide. And don't you mess up my room. But why did you abandon it? That's a sin.

GRUSHA *looking out of the window:* There, they're coming from behind the trees. I shouldn't have run away. That gave them ideas. What on earth shall I do?

THE PEASANT WOMAN *looking out of the window and suddenly starting with fear:* Jesus and Mary! Ironshirts!

GRUSHA: They're after the child!

THE PEASANT WOMAN: But suppose they come in!

GRUSHA: You mustn't give it to them. Say it's yours.

THE PEASANT WOMAN: Yes.

GRUSHA: They'll run it through if you let them have it.

THE PEASANT WOMAN: But suppose they demand it? The money for the harvest is in the house.

GRUSHA: If you let them have it, they'll run it through, here in your room! You've got to say it's yours.

THE PEASANT WOMAN: Yes, but suppose they don't believe me?

GRUSHA: You must speak firmly.

THE PEASANT WOMAN: They'll burn the roof over our head.

GRUSHA: That's why you've got to say it's yours. His name's Michael. I shouldn't have told you that.

The peasant woman nods.

Don't nod your head like that. And don't tremble; they'll notice.

THE PEASANT WOMAN: Yes.

GRUSHA: Stop saying yes. I can't stand it any longer. *She shakes her.* Haven't *you* got a child?

THE PEASANT WOMAN *muttering:* In the war.

GRUSHA: Then perhaps he's an Ironshirt, too, by now? And what if he ran children through? You'd give him a fine piece of your mind! 'Stop waving that lance in my room! Is that what I've reared you for? Go and wash your neck before you speak to your mother.'

THE PEASANT WOMAN: That's true, I wouldn't let him behave like that.

GRUSHA: Promise me you'll say it's yours.

THE PEASANT WOMAN: Yes

GRUSHA: There! They're coming!

There is a knocking at the door. The women don't answer. Enter the Ironshirts. The peasant woman bows deeply.

THE CORPORAL: Well, there she is. What did I tell you? My nose. I smelled her. Young lady, I have a question to ask you: Why did you run away? What did you think I would do to you? I'll bet it was something lewd. Confess!

GRUSHA *while the peasant woman continues to bow:* I'd left the milk on the stove. Then I suddenly remembered it.

THE CORPORAL: I thought it was because you imagined I'd looked at you in a lewd way—as if I were thinking there could be something between us. A lustful glance, know what I mean?

GRUSHA: I didn't see that.

THE CORPORAL: But it could have been, eh? You must admit that. After all, I could be a swine. I'm quite frank with you: I could think of all sorts of things if we were alone. *To the peasant woman:* Haven't you got something to do in the yard? The chickens to feed?

THE PEASANT WOMAN *falling suddenly to her knees:* Soldier, I didn't known anything about it. Please don't set my house on fire.

THE CORPORAL: What are you talking about?

THE PEASANT WOMAN: I have nothing to do with it. She left it on the doorstep, I swear.

THE CORPORAL *suddenly sees the child and whistles:* Ah, there's a little one in the crib! Blockhead, I smell a thousand piastres. Take the old girl out and hold on to her. It looks as though I'll have to do some cross-examining.

The peasant woman lets herself be led out by the soldier, without a word.

Well, there's the child I wanted to have from you. *He walks towards the crib.*

GRUSHA: Officer, it's mine. It's not the one you're after.

THE CORPORAL: I'll just have a look at it. *He bends over the crib. Grusha looks round in despair.*

GRUSHA: It's mine! It's mine!

THE CORPORAL: Nice linen!

Grusha jumps at him to pull him away. He throws her off and again bends over the crib. Looking round in despair, she suddenly

lights go down quickly

sees a big log of wood, seizes it in panic, and hits the Corporal over the head from behind. She quickly picks up the child and dashes off.

THE SINGER
> After her escape from the Ironshirts
> After twenty-two days of wandering
> At the foot of the Janga-Tau glacier
> From this moment Grusha Vachnadze decided to be the
>   child's mother.

THE MUSICIANS
> The helpless girl
> Became the mother of the helpless child.
> *Grusha squats over a half-frozen stream to ladle some water in her
> hand for the child.*

GRUSHA
> Nobody wants to take you
> So I shall have to take you
> There is no-one else but me, my dear
> On this black day in a meagre year
> Who will not forsake you.
>
> Since I've carried you too long
> And with sore feet
> Since the milk was too dear
> I grew fond of you.
> (I wouldn't be without you any more.)
>
> I'll throw your fine little shirt away
> And wrap you in rags
> I'll wash you and christen you
> With glacier water.
> (You'll have to bear it.)

She has taken off the child's fine linen and wrapped it in a rag.

THE SINGER
> When Grusha Vachnadze, pursued by the Ironshirts
> Came to the narrow footbridge of the Eastern slope
> She sang the song of the rotten bridge
> And risked two lives.

lights on the floor to look like water

A wind has risen. The bridge on the glacier is visible in the semi-darkness. One rope is broken, and half the bridge is hanging down the precipice. Merchants, two men and a woman, stand undecided before the bridge as Grusha and the child arrive. One man is trying to retrieve a hanging rope with a stick.

THE FIRST MAN: Take your time, young woman. You won't get over that pass anyway.

GRUSHA: But I simply have to get my child over to the east side. To my brother.

THE MERCHANT WOMAN: Have to? What d'you mean by have to? I have to get there, too—because I have to buy two carpets in Atum—carpets a woman had to sell because her husband had to die. But can I do what I have to; can she? Andrei has been fishing for two hours for that rope. And I ask you, how are we to fasten it, even if he gets it?

THE FIRST MAN *listening:* Shush, I think I hear something.

GRUSHA: The bridge is not quite rotten. I think I'll try and cross it.

THE MERCHANT WOMAN: I wouldn't try that even if the devil himself were after me. It's suicide.

THE FIRST MAN *shouting:* Hi!

GRUSHA: Don't shout! *To the merchant woman.* Tell him not to shout.

THE FIRST MAN: But someone down there's calling. Perhaps they've lost their way.

THE MERCHANT WOMAN: And why shouldn't he shout? Is there something wrong with you? Are they after you?

GRUSHA: Well, I'll have to tell you. Ironshirts are after me. I knocked one down.

THE SECOND MAN: Hide our merchandise!

The woman hides a sack behind a rock.

THE FIRST MAN: Why didn't you tell us that at once? *To the other:* If they catch her they'll make mincemeat out of her!

GRUSHA: Get out of my way. I've got to cross that bridge.

THE SECOND MAN: You can't. There's a precipice of two thousand feet.

THE FIRST MAN: Even if we could get the rope it wouldn't
    make sense. We could hold it with our hands, but then the
    Ironshirts could get across in the same way.
GRUSHA: Out of my way.
    Shouts from a distance: 'Let's get up there!'
THE MERCHANT WOMAN: They're getting near. But you
    can't take the child across that bridge. It's sure to break.
    Just look down!
    *Grusha looks down the precipice. The Ironshirts are heard shouting
    below.*
THE SECOND MAN: Two thousand feet!
GRUSHA: But those men are worse.
THE FIRST MAN: Anyway you can't do it with the child. Risk
    your own life if they are after you, but not the child's.
THE SECOND MAN: She's even heavier with the child.
THE MERCHANT WOMAN: Perhaps she's really got to go.
    Give it to me. I'll hide it and you cross the bridge alone.
GRUSHA: I won't. We belong together. *To the child:* Live
    together, die together. *She sings:*

> If the gulf is deep
> And the rotten bridge sways
> It is not for us, son
> To choose our ways.
>
> The way that I know
> Is the one for your feet
> The bread that I find
> Is all you will eat.
>
> Of every four morsels
> You shall have three.
> I would that I knew
> How big they will be!

I'll try it.
THE MERCHANT WOMAN: That's tempting God.
    Shouts from beneath.

GRUSHA: I beg you, throw that stick away, or they'll get the rope and follow me.

She starts off on to the swinging bridge. The merchant woman screams when the bridge looks like breaking. But Grusha walks on and reaches the far side.

THE FIRST MAN: She's done it!

THE MERCHANT WOMAN *who has fallen on her knees and begun to pray, angrily:* But I still think it was a sin.

The Ironshirts appear, the Corporal's head bandaged.

THE CORPORAL: Have you seen a woman with a child?

THE FIRST MAN *while the second throws away his stick:* Yes, there she is! But the bridge won't carry you!

THE CORPORAL: Blockhead, you'll suffer for this!

Grusha, from the far bank, laughs and shows the child to the Ironshirts. She walks on. The bridge is left behind. Wind.

GRUSHA *to the child:* You mustn't mind the wind. It's only a poor wretch, too. It has to push the clouds, and it feels the cold more than any of us. *Snow starts falling.* And the snow isn't the worst, Michael. It covers the little fir trees, so that they won't die in winter. And now I'll sing you a little song. Listen! *She sings:*

> Your father's a thief
> Your mother's a whore:
> All the nice people
> Will love you therefore.
>
> The son of the tiger
> Brings the foals their feed
> The snake-child milk
> To mothers in need.

4

IN THE NORTHERN MOUNTAINS

THE SINGER
Seven days the sister wandered.
Across the glacier, down the hills she wandered.
'When I enter my brother's house', she thought to herself
'He will rise and embrace me'.
'Is that you, sister?' he will say
'I have been expecting you for so long. This here is my
    dear wife.
And this is my farm, come to me by marriage.
With eleven horses and thirty-one cows. Sit down.
Sit down with your child at our table and eat.'
The brother's house was in a lovely valley.
When the sister came to the brother she was ill from her
    wanderings.
The brother rose from the table.

*A fat peasant couple who have just sat down to a meal. Lavrenti
Vachnadze already has a napkin round his neck, as Grusha, pale
and supported by a stableman, enters with the child.*

LAVRENTI: Where do you come from, Grusha?

GRUSHA *feebly:* I've walked across the Janga-Tau Pass,
Lavrenti.

STABLEMAN: I found her in front of the hay barn. She has a
child with her.

THE SISTER-IN-LAW: Go and groom the roan. *Exit stableman.*

LAVRENTI: This is my wife, Aniko.

THE SISTER-IN-LAW: We thought you were in service in
Nukha.

GRUSHA *barely able to stand:* Yes, I was there.

THE SISTER-IN-LAW: Wasn't it a good job? We were told it
was a good one.

GRUSHA: The Governor has been killed.

LAVRENTI: Yes, we heard there were riots. Your aunt told us about it. Remember, Aniko?

THE SISTER-IN-LAW: Here, with us, it's quiet. City people always need some kind of excitement. *She walks towards the door and shouts:* Sosso, Sosso, take the flat cake out of the oven, d'you hear? Where are you? *Exit, shouting.*

LAVRENTI *quietly, quickly:* Has it got a father? *As she shakes her head:* I thought so. We must think up something. She's very pious.

THE SISTER-IN-LAW *returning:* These servants! *To Grusha:* You have a child?

GRUSHA: It's mine. *She collapses. Lavrenti helps her up.*

THE SISTER-IN-LAW: Mary and Joseph, she's ill—what are we to do?

Lavrenti tries to lead Grusha to the bench by the stove. Aniko waves her away in horror and points to the sack by the wall.

LAVRENTI *escorting her to the wall:* Sit down, sit down. I think it's just weakness.

THE SISTER-IN-LAW: As long as it's not scarlet fever.

LAVRENTI: Then she'd have spots. I'm sure it's only weakness. Don't worry, Aniko. *To Grusha:* Do you feel better sitting?

THE SISTER-IN-LAW: Is the child hers?

GRUSHA: It's mine.

LAVRENTI: She's on her way to her husband.

THE SISTER-IN-LAW: Really? Your meat's getting cold. *Lavrenti sits down and begins to eat.* Cold food's not good for you. At least the fat parts mustn't get cold; you know your stomach's your weak spot. *To Grusha:* If your husband's not in town, where is he then?

LAVRENTI: She got married on the other side of the mountain, she says.

THE SISTER-IN-LAW: Oh, on the other side. *She also sits down to eat.*

GRUSHA: I think I'll have to lie down somewhere, Lavrenti.

THE SISTER-IN-LAW *goes on questioning her:* If it's consumption we'll all get it. Has your husband a farm?

GRUSHA: He's a soldier.

LAVRENTI: But he's coming into a farm—a small farm from his father.

THE SISTER-IN-LAW: Isn't he in the war? Why not?

GRUSHA *wearily*: Yes, he's in the war.

THE SISTER-IN-LAW: Then why d'you want to go to the farm?

LAVRENTI: When he comes back from the war, he'll come to his farm.

THE SISTER-IN-LAW: But you're going there now?

LAVRENTI: Yes, to wait for him.

THE SISTER-IN-LAW *shrilly*: Sosso, the cake!

GRUSHA *murmurs in fever*: A farm—a soldier—waiting—sit down—eat.

THE SISTER-IN-LAW: That's scarlet fever.

GRUSHA *starting up*: Yes, he has a farm!

LAVRENTI: I think it must be weakness, Aniko. Wouldn't you like to go and look after the cake yourself, my dear?

THE SISTER-IN-LAW: But when will he come back if the war, as they say, has broken out again? *Waddling away, shouting*: Sosso! Where are you? Sosso!

LAVRENTI *getting up quickly and going to Grusha*: You'll get a bed in a moment. She has a good heart. But only after supper.

GRUSHA *holding out the child to him*: Take it. *He takes it, looking anxiously round.*

LAVRENTI: But you can't stay here long. You must realize she's very pious.

Grusha collapses. Lavrenti takes hold of her.

THE SINGER

>The sister was too ill.
>The cowardly brother had to give her shelter.
>The autumn passed, the winter came.
>The winter was long
>The winter was short.
>The people mustn't know.
>The rats mustn't bite
>The spring mustn't come.

Grusha sits bent at the weaving loom in the scullery. She and the child, who squats on the floor, are wrapped in blankets.
GRUSHA *sings while weaving:*
> Then the lover started to leave
> Then his girl ran pleading after him
> Pleading and crying, crying and pleading:
> Dearest mine, dearest mine
> As you now go into battle
> As you now have to fight the enemy
> Don't throw yourself into the front line
> And don't push with the rear line.
> In front is red fire
> In the rear is red smoke.
> Stay wisely in between
> Keep near the standard bearer.
> The first ones always die
> The last ones are also hit
> Those in the centre come home.

Michael, we must be clever. If we make ourselves really small, like cockroaches, our sister-in-law will forget we're in the house. Then we can stay here till the snow melts. And don't cry because of the cold. Being poor and cold as well puts people off.
Enter Lavrenti. He sits down beside Grusha.
LAVRENTI: Why are you two sitting there muffled up like coachmen? Perhaps it's too cold in the room?
GRUSHA *hastily removing her shawl:* It's not too cold, Lavrenti.
LAVRENTI: If it's too cold, you oughtn't to sit here with the child. Aniko would blame herself. *Pause.* I hope the priest didn't question you about the child.
GRUSHA: He did, but I didn't tell him anything.
LAVRENTI: That's good. I wanted to talk to you about Aniko. She has a good heart—but she's very, very sensitive. People only have to mention our farm and she's worried. She takes everything to heart, you know. Our milkmaid once went to church with a hole in her stocking. Ever since then my

dear Aniko has always worn two pairs of stockings to church. It's hard to believe, but it's the old family in her. *He listens.* Are you sure there are no rats here? If so, you couldn't stay here. *Sounds of drops from the roof.* What's that dripping?

GRUSHA: Must be a barrel leaking.

LAVRENTI: Yes, it must be a barrel. Now you've already been here six months, haven't you? Was I talking about Aniko? Of course I didn't mention the Ironshirt. She has a weak heart. That's why she doesn't know you can't look for work. And that's why she made those remarks yesterday. *They listen again to the melting snow.* Can you believe it? She's worrying about your soldier. 'Suppose he comes back and doesn't find her!' she says, and lies awake. 'He can't come before the spring,' I tell her. The dear woman! *The drops begin to fall faster.* When d'you think he'll come? What's your idea? *Grusha is silent.* Not before the spring. That's what you think, too? *Grusha is silent.* I see you no longer believe he'll come back. *Grusha does not answer.* But when spring comes and the snow is melting on the passes you must leave here. Because then they can come and look for you. People are already talking about a child with an un-married mother.

The beat of the falling drops has grown faster and steadier.

Grusha, the snow is melting on the roof and spring is here.

GRUSHA: Yes.

LAVRENTI *eagerly:* Let me tell you what we'll do. You need a place to go to. And because of the child—*he sighs*—you must have a husband, to stop people talking. I've made cautious inquiries about how we can get a husband for you, Grusha, and I've found one. I talked to a woman who has a son, just over the mountain, a little farm. She's willing.

GRUSHA: But I can't marry another man! I must wait for Simon Chachava.

LAVRENTI: Of course. That's all been considered. You don't need a man in bed, but a man on paper. And that's the very

man I've found. The son of the woman I spoke to is dying.
Isn't that wonderful? He's just at his last gasp. And every-
thing's as we have said: A man just over the mountain!
And when you reached him he died, and so you're a widow.
What do you say?

GRUSHA: I could do with a stamped up document for Michael.

LAVRENTI: A stamp makes all the difference. Without a
stamp even the Shah of Persia couldn't prove he is the
Shah. And you'll have a roof over your head.

GRUSHA: How much does she want for it?

LAVRENTI: 400 piastres.

GRUSHA: Where will you find the money?

LAVRENTI *guiltily:* Aniko's milk money.

GRUSHA: No-one will know us over there. I'll do it.

LAVRENTI *gets up:* I'll tell the woman at once. *Exit quickly.*

GRUSHA: Michael, you cause a lot of trouble. I came by you
as the pear tree comes by the sparrows. And because a
Christian bends down and picks up a crust of bread so it
won't go to waste. Michael, I ought to have walked away
quickly on that Easter Sunday in Nukha. Now I'm the fool.

THE SINGER

The bridegroom was lying on his deathbed, when the
bride arrived.

The bridegroom's mother was waiting at the door,
bidding them hurry.

The bride brought along a child, the witness hid it during
the wedding.

*A space divided by a partition. On one side a bed. Under the
mosquito net lies a very sick man. On the other side the mother-in-
law rushes in pulling Grusha after her. They are followed by
Lavrenti and the child.*

THE MOTHER-IN-LAW: Quick! Quick! Or he'll die on us
before the wedding. *To Lavrenti:* But I was never told she
already had a child.

LAVRENTI: What's it matter? *Pointing towards the dying man:*
It's all the same to him in his condition.

THE MOTHER-IN-LAW: Him? But I won't survive the shame. We're honest people. *She begins to weep.* My Yussup doesn't have to marry someone who already has a child.

LAVRENTI: All right, I'll add another 200 piastres. You have it in writing that the farm will go to you; but she has the right to live here for two years.

THE MOTHER-IN-LAW *drying her tears:* It will hardly cover the funeral expenses. I hope she will really lend me a hand with the work. And now what's happened to the monk? He must have slipped out by the kitchen window. When they get wind in the village that Yussup's end is near, they'll all be round our necks. Oh dear! I'll go and get the monk. But he mustn't see the child.

LAVRENTI: I'll take care he doesn't see it. But why a monk? Why not a priest?

THE MOTHER-IN-LAW: Oh, he's just as good. I made one mistake: I paid him half his fee in advance. Now he'll have gone to the tavern. I hope . . . *She runs off.*

LAVRENTI: She saved on the priest, the wretch! She's hired a cheap monk.

GRUSHA: Send Simon Chachava to me if he turns up.

LAVRENTI: Yes. *Glancing at the sick man:* Won't you have a look at him?

Grusha, taking Michael to her, shakes her head.

He's not moving an eyelid. I hope we aren't too late.

They listen. On the opposite side enter neighbours, who look round and take up positions against the walls. They start muttering prayers. Enter the mother-in-law with the monk.

THE MOTHER-IN-LAW *surprised and angry, to the monk:* Now we're for it! *She bows to the guests.* I must ask you to wait a few moments. My son's bride has just arrived from town and we've got to have an emergency wedding. *She goes with the monk into the bedchamber.* I knew you'd spread it about. *To Grusha:* The wedding can start at once. Here's the licence. I and the bride's brother—*Lavrenti tries to hide in the background, after having quickly taken Michael away from Grusha.*

The mother-in law beckons him away from the child—the bride's brother and I are the witnesses.

Grusha has bowed to the monk. They approach the bed: the mother-in-law lifts the mosquito-net: the monk begins babbling the marriage service in Latin. Meanwhile the mother-in-law beckons to Lavrenti to get rid of the child, but Lavrenti, fearing that the child will cry, draws its attention to the ceremony. Grusha glances once at the child, and Lavrenti makes the child wave to her.

THE MONK: Are you prepared to be a faithful, obedient and good wife to this man? And to cleave to him until death you do part?

GRUSHA *looking at the child:* Yes.

THE MONK *to the dying man:* And are you prepared to be a good and loving husband to your wife until death you do part? *As the dying man does not answer, the monk repeats the question, then looks round.*

THE MOTHER-IN-LAW: Of course he is! Didn't you hear him say yes?

THE MONK: All right. We declare this marriage contracted. Now what about Extreme Unction?

THE MOTHER-IN-LAW: Nothing doing! The wedding was quite expensive enough. I must now take care of the mourners. *To Lavrenti:* Did we say 700?

LAVRENTI: 600. *He pays.* Now I don't want to sit and get acquainted with the guests. So farewell, Grusha. And if my widowed sister comes to visit me one day, she'll get a 'welcome' from my wife. Or I'll get disagreeable.

He leaves. The mourners glance after him without interest.

THE MONK: And may one ask whose this child is?

THE MOTHER-IN-LAW: Is there a child? I don't see any child. And you don't see one either—understand? Or else I've seen all kinds of things happening behind the tavern! Come along now.

They move back to the room. After Grusha has put down the child and told it to be quiet, she is introduced to the neighbours.

This is my daughter-in-law. She arrived just in time to find dear Yussup still alive.

ONE OF THE WOMEN: He's been ill now a whole year, hasn't he? When my Vassili was called up he was there to say goodbye.

ANOTHER WOMAN: Such things are terrible for a farm. With the corn ripe on the stalk and the farmer in bed! It will be a blessing for him if he doesn't suffer much longer, I say.

FIRST WOMAN *confidentially:* At first we thought he took to his bed because of military service, you know. And now his end is coming.

THE MOTHER-IN-LAW: Please sit down and have some cakes. *She beckons to Grusha and both women go into the bedroom, where they pick up trays of cakes from the floor. The guests, among them the monk, sit on the floor and begin conversing in subdued voices.*

A VERY OLD PEASANT *to whom the monk has slipped the bottle he has taken from his cassock:* There's a little one, you say! How can Yussup have managed that?

THIRD WOMAN: Anyway, she was lucky to have brought it off in time, with him so sick.

THE MOTHER-IN-LAW: They are gossiping already. And stuffing themselves with the funeral cakes at the same time. And if he doesn't die today, I'll have to bake fresh ones tomorrow.

GRUSHA: I'll bake them.

THE MOTHER-IN-LAW: When some riders passed by last night, and I went out to see who they were, he was lying there like a corpse! That's why I sent for you. It can't take much longer. *She listens.*

THE MONK: Dear wedding guests and mourners! We stand deeply moved in front of a bed of death and marriage, because the bride gets into bed and the groom into the grave. The groom is already washed, and the bride is already hot. For in the marriage-bed lies the last Will, and that makes people randy. Oh, my children, how varied is the fate of man! The one dies to get a roof over his head, and the other marries so that flesh may be turned to dust, from which it was made. Amen.

THE MOTHER-IN-LAW *who had listened:* He's got his own

back. I shouldn't have hired such a cheap one. That's what you'd expect. An expensive one knows how to behave. In Sura there's one who is even in the odour of sanctity; but of course he charges a fortune. A fifty-piastre priest like this one here has no dignity. And as for piety, he has precisely fifty piastres' worth, and no more. And when I fetched him from the tavern he was just finishing a speech and shouting: 'The war is over, beware of the peace!' We must go in.

GRUSHA *giving Michael a cake:* Eat this cake and be a good boy, Michael. We are respectable now.

The two women carry the trays of cakes to the guests. The dying man is sitting up in bed; he puts his head out from under the mosquito-net and watches the two women. Then he sinks back again. The monk takes two bottles from his cassock and offers them to the peasant beside him. Enter three musicians, to whom the monk waves with a grin.

THE MOTHER-IN-LAW *to the musicians:* What have you got your instruments for?

A MUSICIAN: Brother Anastasius here—*pointing at the monk*—told us there was a wedding going on.

THE MOTHER-IN-LAW: What! You brought them? Three more on my neck! Don't you know there's a dying man next door?

THE MONK: That's a tempting task for an artist. They could play a hushed Wedding March or a gay Funeral Dance.

THE MOTHER-IN-LAW: Well, you might as well play. I can't stop you eating, in any case.

The musicians play a musical medley. The women offer cakes.

THE MONK: The trumpet sounds like a whining baby. And you, little drum, what gossip are you spreading abroad?

A PEASANT *beside the monk:* What about the bride shaking a leg?

THE MONK: Shake the legs or rattle the bones?

THE PEASANT *beside the monk, singing:*
When pretty Miss Plushbottom wed
A rich man with no teeth in his head

They enquired, 'Is it fun?'
She replied, 'No, it's none.
Still, there're candles and soon he'll be dead.'
*The mother-in-law throws the drunken man out. The music stops.
The guests are embarrassed. Pause.*

THE GUESTS *loudly:* Have you heard the latest? The Grand
Duke's back!—But the Princes are against him.—Oh, the
Shah of Persia, they say, has lent him a great army, to
restore order in Grusinia.—How is this possible? After all,
the Shah of Persia is against the Grand Duke!—But against
disorder, too.—In any case, the war's over. Our soldiers
are already coming back.

Grusha drops the tray of cakes.

AN OLD WOMAN *to Grusha:* Are you feeling ill? That's just
excitement about dear Yussup. Sit down and rest awhile,
my dear.

Grusha stands, swaying.

THE GUESTS: Now everything will be as it was. Only the taxes
will go up because we'll have to pay for the war.

GRUSHA *weakly:* Did someone say the soldiers are back?

A MAN: I did.

GRUSHA: That can't be true.

THE MAN *to a woman:* Show her the shawl. We bought it
from a soldier. It's from Persia.

GRUSHA *looking at the shawl:* They are here.

*A long pause. Grusha kneels as if to pick up the cakes. As she does
so she takes the silver cross and chain out of her blouse, kisses it, and
starts praying.*

THE MOTHER-IN-LAW *while the guests silently watch Grusha:*
What's the matter with you? Won't you look after our
guests? What's all this nonsense from the city got to do
with us?

THE GUESTS *resuming their conversation while Grusha remains with
her forehead bent to the ground:* Persian saddles can be bought
from soldiers, but some exchange them for crutches.—
Only one side's bigwigs can win, but the soldiers on
both sides are the losers.—At least the war's over now.

It's something that they can't call you up any more.—*The dying man sits bolt upright in bed. He listens.*—What we need most are two weeks of good weather.—There's hardly a pear on our trees this year.

THE MOTHER-IN-LAW *offering the cakes:* Have some more cake. And enjoy it. There's more to come.

The mother-in-law goes to the bedroom with empty trays. Unaware of the dying man, she bends down to pick up some more cakes, when he begins to talk in a hoarse voice.

YUSSUP: How many more cakes are you going to stuff down their throats? D'you think I can shit money? *The mother-in-law starts, and stares at him aghast, while he puts his head out from behind the mosquito-net.* Did they say the war was over?

FIRST WOMAN *talking kindly to Grusha in the next room:* Has the young woman someone in the war?

THE MAN: That's good news that they're on their way home, eh?

YUSSUP: Don't stare so! Where's the wife you've foisted on me?

Receiving no answer, he climbs out of bed and in his nightshirt staggers past his mother into the other room. Trembling, she follows him with the cake tray.

THE GUESTS *seeing him and shrieking:* Jesus, Mary and Joseph! Yussup!

Everyone leaps up in alarm. The women rush to the door. Grusha, still on her knees, turns round and stares at the man.

YUSSUP: The funeral supper! That's what you'd like! Get out before I kick you out!

The guests stampede from the house.

YUSSUP *grumpily to Grusha:* That puts a spoke in your wheel, eh?

Receiving no answer, he turns round and takes a cake from the tray which his mother holds.

THE SINGER

Oh, confusion! The wife discovers that she has a husband!

By day there's the child, by night there's the man.

The lover is on his way day and night.
The married couple are looking at each other. The
chamber is narrow.

*Yussup sits naked in a high wooden bathtub. His mother pours
water from a jug. Next door in the bedroom Grusha squats with
Michael, who is playing at mending a straw mat.*

YUSSUP: That's her business, not yours. Where's she hiding
now?

THE MOTHER-IN-LAW *calling:* Grusha! The peasant wants
you!

GRUSHA *to Michael:* There are still two holes to mend.

YUSSUP *as Grusha enters:* Scrub my back!

GRUSHA: Can't the peasant do that himself?

YUSSUP: 'Can't the peasant do that himself?' Get the brush!
To hell with you! Are you the wife or are you a stranger?
To the mother-in-law: Too cold!

THE MOTHER-IN-LAW: I'll run and get some more hot
water.

GRUSHA: Let me do it.

YUSSUP: You stay here. *The mother-in-law goes out.* Rub harder.
And don't make such a fuss. You've seen a naked man before. That child of yours can't have come out of thin air.

GRUSHA: The child was not conceived in joy, if that's what
the peasant means.

YUSSUP *turning and grinning:* A likely story! *Grusha stops scrub-
bing him and starts back. Enter the mother-in-law.* This is a
nice thing you've saddled me with here! A cold-fish for
a wife!

THE MOTHER-IN-LAW: She isn't willing.

YUSSUP: Pour—but go easy! Ow! Go easy, I said. *To Grusha.*
I'd be surprised if you hadn't been up to something in the
city. What else would you be here for? But I won't say
anything about that. I also haven't said anything about the
bastard you brought into my house. But my patience with
you is coming to an end. It's against nature. *To the
mother-in-law:* More! *To Grusha:* And even if your soldier
does return, you're married.

GRUSHA: Yes.

YUSSUP: But your soldier won't return now. Don't you believe it.

GRUSHA: No.

YUSSUP: You're cheating me. You're my wife and you're not my wife. Where you lie, nothing lies. And yet no other woman can lie there. When I go to work in the mornings I'm dead-tired. When I lie down at night I'm awake as the devil. God has made you a woman, and what d'you do about it? My fields don't bring me in enough to buy myself a woman in town. Besides, it's a long way. Woman hoes the fields and parts her legs. That's what our almanac says. D'you hear?

GRUSHA: Yes. *Quietly.* I don't like cheating you out of it.

YUSSUP: She doesn't like! Pour some more water. *The mother-in-law pours.* Ow!

THE SINGER

As she sat by the stream to wash the linen
She saw his image in the water, and his face grew dimmer
As the months passed by.
As she raised herself to wring the linen
She heard his voice from the murmuring maple, and his
    voice grew fainter
As the months passed by.
Excuses and sighs grew more numerous, tears and sweat
    flowed faster
As the months passed by, as the child grew up.

Grusha sits by a stream dipping linen into the water. Some distance away a few children are standing. Grusha is talking to Michael.

GRUSHA: You can play with them, Michael. But don't let them order you about because you're the smallest.

Michael nods and joins the children. They start playing.

THE TALLEST BOY: Today we're going to play Heads-off. *To a fat boy:* You're the Prince and you must laugh. *To Michael:* You're the Governor. *To a girl:* You're the Governor's wife and you cry when his head's chopped off. And I do the chopping. *He shows his wooden sword.* With this. First, the Governor's led into the courtyard. The Prince walks ahead. The Governor's wife comes last.

They form a procession. The fat boy goes ahead, and laughs. Then comes Michael, and the tallest boy, and then the girl, who weeps.

MICHAEL *standing still:* Me too chop head off!

THE TALLEST BOY: That's my job. You're the smallest. The Governor's part is easiest. All you do is kneel down and have your head chopped off. That's simple.

MICHAEL: Me too have sword.

THE TALLEST BOY: That's mine. *He gives him a kick.*

THE GIRL *shouting to Grusha:* He doesn't want to do what he's told.

GRUSHA *laughing:* Even ducklings take to water, they say.

THE TALLEST BOY: You can play the Prince if you know how to laugh.

Michael shakes his head.

THE FAT BOY: I'm the best laugher. Let him chop off the head just once. Then you do it, then me.

Reluctantly the tallest boy hands Michael the wooden sword and kneels. The fat boy sits down, smacks his thigh and laughs with all his might. The girl weeps loudly. Michael swings the big sword and chops off the head. In doing so, he topples over.

THE TALLEST BOY: Hi, I'll show you how to do it properly.

Michael runs away, and the children run after him. Grusha laughs, following them with her eyes. On turning round, she sees Simon Chachava standing on the opposite bank. He wears a shabby uniform.

GRUSHA: Simon!

SIMON: Is that Grusha Vachnadze?

GRUSHA: Simon!

SIMON *politely:* A good morning, and good health to the young lady.

GRUSHA *gets up gaily and bows deeply:* A good morning to the soldier. And thank God he has returned in good health.

SIMON: They found better fish than me, so they didn't eat me, said the haddock.

GRUSHA: Courage, said the kitchen boy. Luck, said the hero.

SIMON: And how are things here? Was the winter bearable? Did the neighbour behave?

GRUSHA: The winter was a little rough, the neighbour as usual, Simon.

SIMON: May one ask if a certain person is still in the habit of putting her leg in the water when washing her linen?

GRUSHA: The answer is no. Because of the eyes in the bushes.

SIMON: The young lady is talking about soldiers. Here stands a paymaster.

GRUSHA: Is that worth twenty piastres?

SIMON: And board.

GRUSHA *with tears in her eyes:* Behind the barracks under the date trees.

SIMON: Just there. I see someone has kept her eyes open.

GRUSHA: Someone has.

SIMON: And has not forgotten. *Grusha shakes her head.* And so the door is still on its hinges, as they say. *Grusha looks at him in silence and shakes her head again.* What's that mean? Is something wrong?

GRUSHA: Simon Chachava, I can never go back to Nukha. Something has happened.

SIMON: What has happened?

GRUSHA: It so happened that I knocked down an Ironshirt.

SIMON: Grusha Vachnadze will have had her reasons for that.

GRUSHA: Simon Chachava, my name is also no longer what it was.

SIMON *after a pause:* I don't understand that.

GRUSHA: When do women change their names, Simon? Let me explain it to you: Nothing stands between us. Everything between us has remained as it was. You've got to believe that.

SIMON: How can nothing stand between us and things be changed?

GRUSHA: How can I explain it to you? So fast and with the stream between us? Couldn't you cross that bridge?

SIMON: Perhaps it's no longer necessary.

GRUSHA: It's most necessary. Come over, Simon. Quick!

SIMON: Is the young lady saying that someone has come too late?

Grusha looks up at him in despair, her face streaming with tears. Simon stares before him. He picks up a piece of wood and starts cutting it.

THE SINGER

So many words are said, so many words are left unsaid.

The soldier has come. Whence he comes he doesn't say.

Hear what he thought but didn't say:

The battle began at dawn, grew bloody at noon.

The first fell before me, the second behind me, the third at my side.

I trod on the first, I abandoned the second, the captain sabred the third.

My one brother died by steel, my other brother died by smoke.

My neck was burnt by fire, my hands froze in my gloves, my toes in my socks.

For food I had aspen buds, for drink I had maple brew, for bed I had stones in water.

SIMON: I see a cap in the grass. Is there a little one already?

GRUSHA: There is, Simon. How could I hide it? But please don't let it worry you. It's not mine.

SIMON: They say: Once the wind begins to blow, it blows through every crack. The woman need say no more.

Grusha lowers her head and says no more.

THE SINGER

There was great yearning but there was no waiting.

The oath is broken. Why was not disclosed.

Hear what she thought, but didn't say:

While you fought in the battle, soldier

The bloody battle, the bitter battle

I found a child who was helpless

And hadn't the heart to do away with it.

I had to care for what otherwise would have come to harm

I had to bend down on the floor for breadcrumbs
I had to tear myself to pieces for what was not mine
But alien.
Someone must be the helper.
Because the little tree needs its water
The little lamb loses its way when the herdsman is asleep
And the bleating remains unheard.

SIMON: Give me back the cross I gave you. Or better, throw
it in the stream.
He turns to go.
GRUSHA: Simon Chachava, don't go away. It isn't mine, it
isn't mine! *She hears the children calling.* What is it, children?
VOICES: Soldiers have come!—They are taking Michael
away!
*Grusha stands aghast as two Ironshirts, with Michael between
them, come towards her.*
IRONSHIRT: Are you Grusha? *She nods.* Is that your child?
GRUSHA: Yes. *Simon goes off.* Simon!
IRONSHIRT: We have official orders to take this child, found
in your charge, back to the city. There is suspicion that it is
Michael Abashvili, son and heir of the late Governor Georgi
Abashvili, and his wife, Natella Abashvili. Here is the
document and the seal.
They lead the child away.
GRUSHA *running after them and shouting:* Leave it here, please!
It's mine!
THE SINGER
The Ironshirts took the child away, the precious child.
The unhappy girl followed them to the city, the danger-
ous place.
The real mother demanded the child back. The foster
mother faced her trial.
Who will try the case, on whom will the child be be-
stowed?
Who will be the Judge? A good one, a bad one?
The city was in flames. On the Judgment Seat sat Azdak.

5

THE STORY OF THE JUDGE

THE SINGER
Listen now to the story of the Judge:
How he turned Judge, how he passed judgment, what
kind of Judge he is.
On the Easter Sunday of the great revolt, when the
Grand Duke was overthrown
And his Governor Abashvili, father of our child, lost his
head
The village clerk Azdak found a fugitive in the woods and
hid him in his hut.

Azdak, in rags and tipsy, helps a fugitive dressed as a beggar into his hut.

AZDAK: Don't snort. You're not a horse. And it won't do you
any good with the police if you run like a dirty nose in
April. Stop, I tell you. *He catches the fugitive, who has trotted
into the hut as though he would go through the walls.* Sit down and
feed: here's a piece of cheese. *From under some rags in a chest
he fishes out some cheese, and the fugitive greedily begins to eat.*
Haven't had anything for some time, eh? *The fugitive groans.*
Why did you run so fast, you arse-hole? The police
wouldn't even have seen you!

THE FUGITIVE: Had to.

AZDAK: Blue funk? *The fugitive stares, uncomprehending.* Got the
squitters? Afraid? Don't slobber like a Grand Duke or a
sow. I can't stand it. It's well-born stinkers we've got to put
up with as God made them. Not the likes of you. I once
heard of a Senior Judge who farted at a public dinner. Just
to show his independence. Watching you eat like that really
gives me the most awful ideas! Why don't you say something? *Sharply.* Let's have a look at your hand. Can't you
hear? Show me your hand. *The fugitive slowly puts out his
hand.* White! So you're no beggar at all! A fraud! A swindle

on legs! And here am I hiding you from the police as though
you were a decent human being! Why run like that if you're
a landowner? Because that's what you are. Don't try to
deny it. I see it in your guilty face. *He gets up.* Get out of
here! *The fugitive looks uncertainly at him.* What are you waiting
for, you peasant-flogger?

THE FUGITIVE: Am hunted. Ask for undivided attention.
Make proposition.

AZDAK: What do you want to make? A proposition? Well, if
that isn't the height of insolence! He making a proposition!
The bitten man scratches his fingers bloody, and the leech
makes a proposition. Get out, I tell you!

THE FUGITIVE: Understand point of view. Persuasion. Will
pay 100,000 piastres for one night. How's that?

AZDAK: What? Do you think you can buy me? And for
100,000 piastres? A third-rate farm. Let's say 150,000. Got
it?

THE FUGITIVE: Not on me, of course. Will be sent. Hope,
don't doubt.

AZDAK: Doubt profoundly! Get out!

The fugitive gets up and trots to the door. A voice from off-stage.

VOICE: Azdak!

The fugitive turns, trots to the opposite corner and stands still.

AZDAK *shouting:* I'm not in. *He walks to the door.* Is that you
spying around here again, Shauva?

POLICEMAN SHAUVA *outside, reproachfully:* You've snared
another rabbit, Azdak. You promised me it wouldn't
happen again.

AZDAK *severely:* Shauva, don't talk about things you don't
understand. The rabbit is a dangerous and destructive
animal. It devours plants, especially what they call weeds.
So it must be exterminated.

SHAUVA: Azdak, don't be so hard on me. I'll lose my job if I
don't arrest you. I know you have a good heart.

AZDAK: I *don't* have a good heart! How often am I to tell you
I'm a man of intellect?

SHAUVA *slyly:* I know, Azdak. You're a superior person. You say so yourself. I'm a Christian and I've no education. So I ask you: if one of the Prince's rabbits is stolen, and I'm a policeman, what am I to do with the offender?

AZDAK: Shauva, Shauva, shame on you! There you stand asking me a question. Nothing is more tempting than a question. Suppose you were a woman—let's say Nunovna, that bad girl—and you showed me your thigh—Nunovna's thigh, that is—and you asked me: what shall I do with my thigh? It itches. Is she as innocent as she pretends? No. I catch a rabbit, you catch a man. Man is made in God's image. Not so a rabbit, you know that. I'm a rabbit-eater; but you're a man-eater, Shauva. And God will pass judgment on you. Shauva, go home and repent. No, stop! There's something . . . *He looks at the fugitive, who stands trembling in the corner.* No, it's nothing after all. Go home and repent. *He slams the door behind Shauva. To the fugitive:* Now you're surprised, eh? Surprised I didn't hand you over? But I couldn't hand over even a bedbug to that beast of a policeman! It goes against my grain. Don't tremble at the sight of a policeman. So old and yet so cowardly! Finish your cheese, but eat it like a poor man, or else they'll still catch you. Do I even have to tell you how a poor man behaves? *He makes him sit down, and then gives him back the cheese.* The box is the table. Put your elbows on the table, and now surround the plate with your arms as though you expected the cheese to be snatched from you at any moment. What right have you to be safe? Now hold the knife as if it were a small sickle; and don't look so greedily at your cheese, look at it mournfully—because it's already disappearing—like all good things. *Azdak watches him.* They're after you. That speaks in your favour. But how can I be sure they're not mistaken about you? In Tiflis they once hanged a landowner, a Turk. He could prove he quartered his peasants instead of merely cutting them in half, as is the custom. And he squeezed twice the usual amount of taxes out of them. His zeal was above all suspicion, and yet they hanged him like a common criminal. Why? Because he was

a Turk—something he couldn't do much about. An in-
justice! He got on to the gallows like Pontius Pilate into
the Creed. In a word, I don't trust you.

THE SINGER
Thus Azdak gave shelter to the old beggar
Only to find out that he was that murderer, the Grand
Duke.
And he was ashamed of himself, he accused himself and
ordered the policeman
To take him to Nukha, to Court, to be judged.
*In the Court of Justice three Ironshirts sit drinking. From a pillar
hangs a man in judge's robes. Enter Azdak, in chains, dragging
Shauva behind him.*
AZDAK *shouting:* I have helped the Grand Duke, the Grand
Thief, the Grand Murderer, to escape! In the name of
Justice, I demand to be judged severely in a public trial!
THE FIRST IRONSHIRT: Who is this queer bird?
SHAUVA: That's our clerk, Azdak.
AZDAK: I am despicable, treacherous, branded! Tell them,
flatfoot, how I insisted on being put in chains and brought
to the capital. Because I sheltered the Grand Duke, the
Grand Swindler, by mistake. As I realized only afterwards
when I found this document in my hut. *The Ironshirts study
the document. To Shauva:* They can't read. Point out that the
branded man is accusing himself. Tell them how I forced
you to walk with me through half the night, to get everything cleared up.
SHAUVA: And all by threats. That wasn't nice of you, Azdak.
AZDAK: Shauva, shut your trap. You don't understand. A
new age has come, which will thunder over you. You're
finished. The police are being wiped out, pfft! Everything
is being investigated, brought into the open. In which
case a man prefers to give himself up. Why? Because he
won't escape the mob. Tell them how I've been shouting
all along Shoemaker Street! *He acts with expansive gestures,
looking sideways at the Ironshirts.* 'Out of ignorance I let the

Grand Swindler escape. Tear me to pieces, brothers!' So as to get in first.

THE FIRST IRONSHIRT: And what was their answer?

SHAUVA: They comforted him in Butcher Street, and laughed themselves sick in Shoemaker Street. That's all.

AZDAK: But here with you it's different, I know you're men of iron. Brothers, where is the Judge? I must be tried.

THE FIRST IRONSHIRT *pointing at the hanged man:* Here's the Judge. And stop 'brothering' us. That's rather a sore spot this evening.

AZDAK: 'Here's the Judge.' That's an answer never heard in Grusinia before. Citizens, where's His Excellency the Governor? *Pointing at the gallows:* Here's His Excellency, stranger. Where's the Chief Tax Collector? Where's the official Recruiting Officer? The Patriarch? The Chief of Police? Here, here, here—all here. Brothers, that's what I expected from you.

THE SECOND IRONSHIRT: Stop! What did you expect, you bird?

AZDAK: What happened in Persia, brothers. What happened there.

THE SECOND IRONSHIRT: And what did happen in Persia?

AZDAK: Forty years ago. Everyone hanged. Viziers, tax-collectors. My grandfather, a remarkable man, saw it all. For three whole days. Everywhere.

THE SECOND IRONSHIRT: And who reigned after the Vizier was hanged?

AZDAK: A peasant.

THE SECOND IRONSHIRT: And who commanded the army?

AZDAK: A soldier, soldier.

THE SECOND IRONSHIRT: And who paid the wages?

ADAZK: A dyer. A dyer paid the wages.

THE SECOND IRONSHIRT: Wasn't it a carpet weaver perhaps?

THE FIRST IRONSHIRT: And why did all this happen, you Persian?

AZDAK: 'Why did all this happen?' Must there be a special

reason? Why do you scratch yourself, brother? War! Too
long a war! And no justice! My grandfather brought back a
song that tells what it was all about. I and my friend the
policeman will sing it for you. *To Shauva:* And hold on to
the rope, that's part of it. *He sings, with Shauva holding the
rope.*

> Why don't our sons bleed any longer, why don't our
> daughters weep any more?
> Why do only the calves in the slaughterhouse have any
> blood, why only willows on Lake Urmi tears?
> The Grand King must have a new province, the peasant
> must relinquish his savings.
> In order to capture the roof of the world, the cottage
> roofs have to be torn down.
> Our men are scattered in all directions, so that the great
> ones can eat at home.
> The soldiers kill each other, the marshals salute each
> other.
> The widow's tax money has to be fingered to see if it's
> good, the swords break.
> The battle has been lost, but the helmets have been paid
> for.
> Is that right? Is that right?

SHAUVA: Yes, yes, yes, yes, yes, that's right.
AZDAK: Do you want to hear the whole thing?
The first Ironshirt nods.
THE SECOND IRONSHIRT *to Shauva:* Did he teach you that
song?
SHAUVA: Yes. Only my voice isn't good.
THE SECOND IRONSHIRT: No. *To Azdak:* Go on singing.
AZDAK: The second verse is about the peace. *He sings:*

> The offices are jammed, the officials are working in the
> streets.
> The rivers overflow their banks and lay waste the fields.
> Those incapable of letting down their own trousers rule
> countries.
> Those who can't count up to four devour eight courses.

The corn farmers look round for buyers, but see only the
   starving.
The weavers go home from their looms in rags.
Is that right? Is that right?
SHAUVA: Yes, yes, yes, yes, yes, that's right.
AZDAK:
   That's why our sons bleed no longer, our daughters weep
      no more.
   That's why only the calves in the slaughterhouse have
      any blood.
   And the willows in the morning on Lake Urmi have any
      tears.
THE FIRST IRONSHIRT *after a pause:* Are you going to sing
   that song here in town?
AZDAK: Of course. What's wrong with it?
THE FIRST IRONSHIRT: Do you see the sky getting red?
   Turning round, Azdak sees the sky reddened by fire. That's in the
   outer town. This morning when Prince Kazbeki had Gover-
   nor Abashvili beheaded our carpet weavers also caught the
   'Persian disease'. They asked if Prince Kazbeki isn't eating
   too many courses. And this afternoon they strung up the
   town judge. But we beat them to pulp for two piastres per
   weaver, you understand?
AZDAK *after a pause:* I understand.
   *He glances shyly round and, creeping away, sits down in a corner, his
   head in his hands.*
THE FIRST IRONSHIRT *to the third, after they have all had a
   drink:* Just wait and see what'll happen next.
   *The first and second Ironshirts walk towards Azdak and block his
   exit.*
SHAUVA: I don't think he's a really bad character, gentlemen.
   He poaches a few chickens here and there, and perhaps an
   odd rabbit.
THE SECOND IRONSHIRT *approaching Azdak:* You've come
   here to fish in troubled waters, eh?
AZDAK *looking up:* I don't know why I've come here.
THE SECOND IRONSHIRT: Do you happen to be in with the

carpet weavers? *Azdak shakes his head.* And what about this song?

AZDAK: From my grandfather. A stupid, ignorant man.

THE SECOND IRONSHIRT: Right. And what about the dyer who paid the wages?

AZDAK: That was in Persia.

THE FIRST IRONSHIRT: And what about denouncing yourself for not having hanged the Grand Duke with your own hands?

AZDAK: Didn't I tell you that I let him escape?

SHAUVA: I swear to it. He let him escape.

The Ironshirts drag Azdak screaming to the gallows. Then they let him loose and burst out laughing. Azdak joins in the laughter, laughing loudest. They then unchain him. They all start drinking. Enter the fat prince with a young man.

THE FIRST IRONSHIRT *to Azdak:* There you have your new age.

More laughter.

THE FAT PRINCE: And what is there to laugh about here, my friends? Permit me a serious word. Yesterday morning the Princes of Grusinia overthrew the Grand Duke's war-thirsty government and did away with his governors. Unfortunately the Grand Duke himself escaped. In this fateful hour our carpet weavers, these eternal trouble-makers, had the audacity to incite a rebellion and hang our universally beloved city Judge, our dear Illa Orbeliani. Tut-tut. My friends, we need peace, peace, peace in Grusinia. And justice. Here I bring you my dear nephew, Bizergan Kazbeki. He's to be the new Judge, a talented fellow. I say: the people must decide.

THE FIRST IRONSHIRT: Does this mean we elect the Judge?

THE FAT PRINCE: Precisely. The people propose a talented fellow. Confer, my friends. *The Ironshirts confer.* Don't worry, little fox. The job's yours. And once we've run the Grand Duke to earth we won't have to kiss the rabble's arse any more.

THE IRONSHIRTS *to each other:* They've got the jitters because they still haven't caught the Grand Duke.—We've this clerk to thank for that. He let him get away.—They're not sure of things yet. So they say: 'My friends!' And: 'The people must decide!'—Now he even wants justice for Grusinia!—But fun's fun as long as it lasts.—We'll ask the clerk; he knows all about justice. Hey, scoundrel . . .

AZDAK: You mean me?

THE FIRST IRONSHIRT *continues:* Would you like to have the nephew as Judge?

AZDAK: You asking me? You're not really asking me that, are you?

THE SECOND IRONSHIRT: Why not? Anything for a laugh!

AZDAK: I take it you want him put to the test? Am I right? Have you a crook on hand? An experienced one? So the candidate can show how good he is?

THE THIRD IRONSHIRT: Let me see. We have the Governor's tarts' two doctors down there. Let's use them.

AZDAK: Stop! That's no good! You can't take real crooks till we're sure of the Judge being appointed. He may be an ass, but he must be appointed or else the law is violated. The law is a very sensitive organ. Like the spleen. Once attacked with fists, death occurs. You can hang those two. Why not? You won't have violated the law, because no Judge was present. Judgment must always be passed with complete solemnity—because it's such rot. Suppose a Judge throws a woman into clink for having stolen a corncake for her child. And he isn't wearing his robes. Or he's scratching himself while passing sentence so that more than a third of his body is exposed—in which case he'd have to scratch his thigh— then the sentence he passes is a disgrace and the law is violated. It would be easier for a Judge's robe and a Judge's hat to pass sentence than for a man without all that para- phernalia. If you don't look out, the law goes up in smoke. You don't taste wine by offering it to a dog. Why not? Because the wine would be gone.

THE FIRST IRONSHIRT: So what do you suggest, you hair-splitter?

AZDAK: I'll be the defendant. I even know what sort. *Azdak whispers to them.*

THE FIRST IRONSHIRT: You? *All burst out laughing.*

THE FAT PRINCE: What have you decided?

THE FIRST IRONSHIRT: We've decided to have a rehearsal. Our good friend will act as defendant, and here's the Judge's seat for the candidate.

THE FAT PRINCE: That's unusual. But why not? *To the nephew:* A mere formality, little fox. What did they teach you? Who gets there first? The slow runner or the fast one?

THE NEPHEW: The silent one, Uncle Arsen.

The nephew sits in the Judge's seat, the fat prince standing behind him. The Ironshirts sit on the steps. Enter Azdak, imitating the unmistakeable gait of the Grand Duke.

AZDAK: Is there anyone here who knows me? I am the Grand Duke.

THE FAT PRINCE: What is he?

THE SECOND IRONSHIRT: The Grand Duke. He really does know him.

THE FAT PRINCE: Good.

THE FIRST IRONSHIRT: Get on with the proceedings.

AZDAK: Listen! I'm accused of war-mongering. Ridiculous! Am saying: ridiculous! Is that enough? If not, have brought lawyers along. About 500. *He points behind him, pretending to be surrounded by lawyers.* Requisition all available seats for lawyers. *The Ironshirts laugh; the fat prince joins in.*

THE NEPHEW *to the Ironshirts:* Do you want me to try this case? I must admit I find it rather unusual. From the point of view of taste, I mean.

THE FIRST IRONSHIRT: Go on.

THE FAT PRINCE *smiling:* Let him have it, little fox!

THE NEPHEW: All right. People of Grusinia versus Grand Duke. What have you to say, defendant?

AZDAK: Any amount. Of course, have myself read war lost. Started war at the time on advice of patriots like Uncle

Kazbeki. Demand Uncle Kazbeki as witness. *The Ironshirts laugh.*

THE FAT PRINCE *to the Ironshirts, affably:* Quite a card, eh?

THE NEPHEW: Motion overruled. You're being accused not of declaring war, which every ruler has to do once in a while, but of conducting it badly.

AZDAK: Rot! Didn't conduct it at all! Had it conducted. Had it conducted by Princes. Made a mess of it, of course.

THE NEPHEW: Do you deny having been Commander in Chief?

AZDAK: Not at all. Always was Commander in Chief. Even at birth ticked off wet-nurse; dismissed turds promptly in potty. Got used to command. Always commanded officials to rob my cash-box. Officers flog soldiers only on my command. Landlords sleep with peasant's wives only when strictly commanded by me. Uncle Kazbeki here grew stomach only on my command.

THE IRONSHIRTS *clapping:* He's good! Up the Grand Duke!

THE FAT PRINCE: Answer him, little fox! I'm with you!

THE NEPHEW: I shall answer him according to the dignity of the law. Defendant, preserve the dignity of the law.

AZDAK: Agreed. Command you proceed with the trial.

THE NEPHEW: It's not your business to command me. So you claim the Princes forced you to declare war. Then how can you claim they made a mess of it?

AZDAK: Didn't send enough troops. Embezzled funds. Brought sick horses. During attack found drunk in whorehouse. Propose Uncle Kaz as witness. *The Ironshirts laugh.*

THE NEPHEW: Are you making the outrageous claim that the Princes of this country did not fight?

AZDAK: No. Princes fought. Fought for war contracts.

THE FAT PRINCE *jumping up:* That's too much! This man talks like a carpet weaver!

AZDAK: Really? Only telling the truth!

THE FAT PRINCE: Hang him! Hang him!

THE FIRST IRONSHIRT: Keep quiet. Get on, Excellency.

THE NEPHEW: Quiet! Now pass sentence. Must be hanged.

Hanged by the neck. Having lost war. Sentence passed. No appeal.

THE FAT PRINCE *hysterically:* Away with him! Away with him! Away with him!

AZDAK: Young man, seriously advise not to fall publicly into jerky, clipped manner of speech. Can't be employed as watchdog if howl like wolf. Got it?

THE FAT PRINCE: Hang him!

AZDAK: If people realize Princes talk same language as Grand Dukes, may even hang Grand Dukes and Princes. By the way, sentence quashed. Reason: war lost, but not for Princes. Princes have won *their* war. Got themselves paid 3,863,000 piastres for horses not delivered.

THE FAT PRINCE: Hang him!

AZDAK: 8,240,000 piastres for food supplies not produced.

THE FAT PRINCE: Hang him!

AZDAK: Are therefore victors. War lost only for Grusinia, which is not present in this Court.

THE FAT PRINCE: I think that's enough, my friends. *To Azdak:* You can withdraw, gaol-bird. *To the Ironshirts:* I think you can now ratify the new Judge's appointment, my friends.

THE FIRST IRONSHIRT: Yes, we can do that. Take down the Judge's robe. *One of the Ironshirts climbs on the back of another and pulls the robe off the hanged man.* And now—to the nephew— you be off so that we can put the right arse on the right seat. *To Azdak:* Step forward, you, and sit on the Judge's seat. *Azdak hesitates.* Sit down up there, man. *Azdak is thrust on to the seat by the Ironshirts.* The Judge was always a rascal. Now the rascal shall be the Judge. *The Judge's robe is placed round his shoulders, the wicker from a bottle on his head.* Look! There's a Judge for you!

THE SINGER

Now there was civil war in the land. The rulers were unsafe.

Now Azdak was made a Judge by the Ironshirts.

Now Azdak remained a Judge for two years.

THE SINGER WITH HIS MUSICIANS
>Great houses turn to ashes
>And blood runs down the street.
>Rats come out of the sewers
>And maggots out of the meat.
>The thug and the blasphemer
>Lounge by the altar-stone:
>Now, now, now Azdak
>Sits on the Judgment throne.

Azdak sits on the Judge's seat peeling an apple. Shauva sweeps out the hall. On one side an invalid in a wheelchair, the accused doctor and a man in rags with a limp; opposite, a young man accused of blackmail. An Ironshirt stands on guard holding the Ironshirts' banner.

AZDAK: In view of the large number of cases, the Court today will hear two cases simultaneously. Before I open the proceedings, a short announcement: I receive—*he stretches out his hand; only the blackmailer produces some money and hands it to him*—I reserve for myself the right to punish one of these parties here—*he glances at the invalid*—for contempt of court. You—*to the doctor*—are a doctor, and you—*to the invalid*—are bringing a complaint against him. Is the doctor responsible for your condition?

THE INVALID: Yes. I had a stroke because of him.

AZDAK: That sounds like professional negligence.

THE INVALID: More than negligence. I gave this man money to study. So far he hasn't paid me back one penny. And when I heard he was treating a patient free, I had a stroke.

AZDAK: Rightly. *To the limping man.* And you, what do you want here?

THE LIMPING MAN: I'm the patient, your Worship.

AZDAK: He treated your leg?

THE LIMPING MAN: Not the right one. My rheumatism was in the left leg, and he operated on my right. That's why I'm limping now.

AZDAK: And you got that free?

THE INVALID: A 500-piastre operation free! For nothing! For a God-Bless-You! And I paid this man's studies! *To the doctor:* Did you learn to operate for nothing at school?

THE DOCTOR *to Azdak:* Your Worship, it is actually the custom to demand the fee before the operation, as the patient is more willing to pay before an operation than after. Which is only human. In this case I was convinced, when I started the operation, that my servant had already received the fee. In this I was mistaken.

THE INVALID: He was mistaken! A good doctor doesn't make mistakes. He examines before he operates.

AZDAK: That's right. *To Shauva:* Public Prosecutor, what's the other case about?

SHAUVA *busily sweeping:* Blackmail.

THE BLACKMAILER: High Court of Justice, I'm innocent. I only wanted to find out from the landowner in question if he really had raped his niece. He kindly informed me that this was not the case, and gave me the money only so that I could let my uncle study music.

AZDAK: Ah ha! *To the doctor:* You on the other hand can't produce any extenuating circumstances in your defence?

THE DOCTOR: Except that to err is human.

AZDAK: And you know that in money matters a good doctor is conscious of his responsibility? I once heard of a doctor who made a thousand piastres out of one sprained finger: he discovered it had something to do with the circulation of the blood, which a less good doctor would have overlooked. On another occasion, by careful treatment, he turned a mediocre gall bladder into a gold mine. You have no excuse, Doctor. The corn merchant Uxu made his son study medicine to get some knowledge of trade—our medical schools are that good. *To the blackmailer:* What's the name of the landowner?

SHAUVA: He doesn't want it to be known.

AZDAK: In that case I will pass judgment. The Court considers the blackmail proved. And you—*to the invalid*—are sentenced to a fine of 1000 piastres. If you get a second stroke the doctor will have to treat you free and if necessary amputate. *To the limping man:* As compensation, you will receive a bottle of embrocation. *To the blackmailer:* You are sentenced to hand over half the proceeds of your deal to the Public Prosecutor, to keep the landowner's name secret. You are advised, moreover, to study medicine. You seem well suited to that profession. And you, Doctor, are acquitted because of an inexcusable professional mistake. The next cases!

THE SINGER WITH HIS MUSICIANS
>Beware of willing Judges
> For Truth is a black cat
>In a windowless room at midnight
> And Justice a blind bat.
>A third and shrugging party
> Alone can right our wrong.
>This, this, this, Azdak
> Does for a mere song.

Enter Azdak from the caravansary on the highway, followed by the old, bearded innkeeper. The Judge's seat is carried by a manservant and Shauva. An Ironshirt with a banner takes up position.

AZDAK: Put it here. Then at least we can get some air and a little breeze from the lemon grove over there. It's good for Justice to do it in the open. The wind blows her skirts up and you can see what's underneath. Shauva, we have eaten too much. These rounds of inspection are very exhausting. *To the innkeeper:* So it's about your daughter-in-law?

THE INNKEEPER: Your Worship, it's about the family honour. I wish to bring an action on behalf of my son, who's gone on business across the mountain. This is the offending stableman, and here's my unfortunate daughter-in-law. *Enter the daughter-in-law, a voluptuous wench. She is veiled.*

AZDAK *sitting down:* I receive. *Sighing, the innkeeper hands him some money.* Good. Now the formalities are disposed of. This is a case of rape?

THE INNKEEPER: Your Worship, I surprised this rascal in the stable in the act of laying our Ludovica in the straw.

AZDAK: Quite right, the stable. Beautiful horses. I particularly like the little roan.

THE INNKEEPER: The first thing I did of course was to berate Ludovica on behalf of my son.

AZDAK *seriously:* I said I liked the little roan.

THE INNKEEPER *coldly:* Really?—Ludovica admitted that the stableman took her against her will.

AZDAK: Take off your veil, Ludovica. *She does so.* Ludovica, you please the Court. Tell us how it happened.

LUDOVICA *as though well rehearsed:* When I entered the stable to look at the new foal, the stableman said to me of his own accord: 'It's hot today' and laid his hand on my left breast. I said to him: 'Don't do that!' But he continued to handle me indecently, which provoked my anger. Before I realized his sinful intentions, he became intimate with me. It had already happened when my father-in-law entered and accidentally trod on me.

THE INNKEEPER *explaining:* On behalf of my son.

AZDAK *to the stableman:* Do you admit that you started it?

THE STABLEMAN: Yes.

AZDAK: Ludovica, do you like to eat sweet things?

LUDOVICA: Yes, sunflower seeds.

AZDAK: Do you like sitting a long time in the tub?

LUDOVICA: Half an hour or so.

AZDAK: Public Prosecutor, just drop your knife on the floor. *Shauwa does so.* Ludovica, go and pick up the Public Prosecutor's knife.

Ludovica, hips swaying, goes and picks up the knife.

Azdak points at her. Do you see that? The way it sways? The criminal element has been discovered. The rape has been proved. By eating too much, especially sweet things, by lying too long in warm water, by laziness and too soft a skin, you have raped the poor man. Do you imagine you can go around with a bottom like that and get away with it in Court? This is a case of deliberate assault with a dangerous weapon. You are sentenced to hand over to the Court the little roan which your father liked to ride on behalf of

his son. And now, Ludovica, come with me to the stable
so that the Court may investigage the scene of the crime.

Azdak is carried on his Judge's seat by Ironshirts from place to
place on the Grusinian highway. Behind him come Shauwa dragging
the gallows and the stableman leading the little roan.

THE SINGER WITH HIS MUSICIANS
> No more did the Lower Orders
> > Tremble in their shoes
> At the bellows of their Betters
> > *At Come-Here's* and *Listen-You's.*
> His balances were crooked
> > But they shouted in the streets:—
> 'Good, good, good is Azdak
> > And the measure that he metes!'

> He took them from Wealthy Peter
> > To give to Penniless Paul
> Sealed his illegal judgments
> > With a waxen tear, and all
> The rag-tag-and-bobtail
> > Ran crying up and down:—
> 'Cheer, cheer, cheer for Azdak
> > The darling of the town!'

The little group slowly withdraws.

> To love your next-door neighbour
> > Approach him with an axe
> For prayers and saws and sermons
> > Are unconvincing facts.
> What miracles of preaching
> > A good sharp blade can do:
> So, so, so, so Azdak
> > Makes miracles come true.

Azdak's Judge's seat is in a tavern. Three farmers stand before
Azdak. Shauwa brings him wine. In a corner stands an old peasant
woman. In the open doorway, and outside, stand villagers and
spectators. An Ironshirt stands guard with a banner.

AZDAK: The Public Prosecutor opens the proceedings.

SHAUVA: It's about a cow. For five weeks the defendant has had a cow in her stable, the property of farmer Suru. She was also found to be in the possession of a stolen ham. And cows belonging to farmer Shutoff were killed after he had asked the defendant to pay the rent for a field.

THE FARMERS: It's about my ham, Your Worship.—It's about my cow, Your Worship.—It's about my field, Your Worship.

AZDAK: Granny, what have you got to say to all this?

THE OLD WOMAN: Your Worship, one night towards morning, five weeks ago, there was a knock at my door, and outside stood a bearded man with a cow. He said, 'Dear woman, I am the miracle-working St Banditus. And because your son has been killed in the war, I bring you this cow as a keepsake. Take good care of it!'

THE FARMERS: The robber Irakli, Your Worship!—Her brother-in-law, Your Worship! The cattle thief, the incendiary!—He must be beheaded!

Outside a woman screams. The crowd grows restless and retreats. Enter the bandit Irakli, with a huge axe.

THE FARMERS: Irakli! *They cross themselves.*

THE BANDIT: A very good evening, dear friends! A glass of wine!

AZDAK: Public Prosecutor, a jug of wine for the guest. And who are you?

THE BANDIT: I'm a wandering hermit, Your Worship. And thank you for the kind gift. *He empties the glass which Shauva has brought.* Same again!

AZDAK: I'm Azdak. *He gets up and bows. The bandit also bows.* The Court welcomes the stranger hermit. Go on with your story, Granny.

THE OLD WOMAN: Your Worship, that first night I didn't know that St Banditus could work miracles, it was only the cow. But one night a few days later the farmer's servants came to take the cow away from me. Then they turned round in front of my door and went off without the cow.

And on their heads sprouted bumps big as a fist. Then I knew that St Banditus had changed their hearts and turned them into friendly people.

The bandit roars with laughter.

THE FIRST FARMER: I know what changed them.

AZDAK: That's good. You can tell us later. Continue.

THE OLD WOMAN: Your Worship, the next one to become a good man was farmer Shutoff—a devil, as everyone knows. But St Banditus brought it about that Shutoff let me off paying the rent for the field.

THE SECOND FARMER: Because my cows were killed in the field.

The bandit laughs.

THE OLD WOMAN *answering Azdak's sign to continue:* And then one morning the ham came flying in at my window. It hit me in the small of the back. I've been lame ever since. Look, Your Worship. *She limps a few steps. The bandit laughs.* I ask Your Worship: when was a poor old body ever given a ham except by a miracle?

The bandit starts sobbing.

AZDAK *rising from his seat:* Granny, that's a question that strikes straight at the Court's heart. Be so kind as to sit down here.

Hesitating, the old woman sits on the Judge's seat. Azdak sits on the floor, glass in hand.

> Little mother, I almost called you Mother Grusinia, the
> woebegone
> The bereaved one, whose sons are in the war.
> Who is beaten with fists, but full of hope.
> Who weeps when she is given a cow
> And is surprised when she is not beaten.
> Little mother, pass merciful sentence on us, the damned!

He bellows to the farmers.

Admit that you don't believe in miracles, you atheists! Each of you is sentenced to pay 500 piastres! For your lack of faith. Get out!

The farmers creep out.

And you, little mother, and you—*to the bandit*—pious man, drink a jug of wine with the Public Prosecutor and Azdak!

THE SINGER WITH HIS MUSICIANS
> To feed the starving people
> > He broke the laws like bread
> There on the seat of justice
> > With the gallows over his head
> For more than seven hundred
> > Days he calmed their wails
> Well, well, well, did Azdak
> > Measure with false scales.

> Two summers and two winters
> > A poor man judged the poor
> And on the wreck of justice
> > He brought them safe to shore
> For he spoke in the mob language
> > That the mob understands.
> I, I, I, cried Azdak
> > Take bribes from empty hands.

THE SINGER
> Then the era of disorder was over, the Grand Duke returned
> The Governor's wife returned, a Judgment was held.
> Many people died, the suburbs burned anew, and fear seized Azdak.

Azdak's Judge's seat stands again in the Court of Justice. Azdak sits on the ground mending a shoe and talking to Shauva. Noises outside. Above a wall the fat prince's head is carried by on a lance.

AZDAK: Shauva, your days of slavery are numbered, perhaps even the minutes. For a long time I have held you on the iron curb of reason, and it has made your mouth bloody. I have lashed you with arguments founded on reason, and ill-treated you with logic. You are by nature a weak creature, and if one slyly throws you an argument, you have to devour it; you can't resist. By nature you are compelled to lick the hand of a superior being, but superior beings can be very different. And now comes your liberation, and you will soon be able to follow your inclinations, which are low. You will be able to follow your unerring instinct, which teaches you to plant your heavy boot on the faces of men. Gone is the era of confusion and disorder, and the great times which I found described in the Song of Chaos have not yet come. Let us now sing that song together in memory of those wonderful days. Sit down and don't violate the music. Don't be afraid. It sounds all right. It has a popular refrain.

He sings

Sister, hide your face; brother, take your knife, the times are out of joint.

The noblemen are full of complaints, the simple folk full of joy.

The city says: let us drive the strong ones out of our midst.

Storm the government buildings, destroy the lists of the serfs.

Now the masters' noses are put to the grindstone. Those who never saw the day have emerged.

The poor-boxes of ebony are broken, the precious sesame wood is used for beds.

He who lacked bread now possesses barns; he who lived on the corn of charity, now measures it out himself.

SHAUVA: Oh, oh, oh, oh.

AZDAK:

Where are you, General? Please, please, please, restore order.

The son of the nobleman can no longer be recognized; the child of the mistress becomes the son of her slave.

The councillors are taking shelter in the barn; he who was barely allowed to sleep on the wall now lolls in bed.

He who once rowed a boat now owns ships; when their owner looks for them, they are no longer his.

Five men are sent out by their master. They say: go yourself, we have arrived.

SHAUVA: Oh, oh, oh, oh.

AZDAK:

Where are you, General? Please, please, please restore order!

Yes, so it might have been, if order had been much longer neglected. But now the Grand Duke, whose life I saved like a fool, has returned to the Capital. And the Persians have lent him an army to restore order. The outer town is already in flames. Go and get me the Big Book I like to sit on. *Shauva brings the book from the Judge's seat. Azdak opens it.* This is the Statute Book and I've always used it, as you can confirm.

SHAUVA: Yes, to sit on.

AZDAK: Now I'd better look and see what they can do to me, because I've always allowed the have-nots to get away with everything. And I'll have to pay for it dearly. I helped to put Poverty on to its rickety legs, so they'll hang me for drunkenness. I peeped into the rich man's pocket, which is considered bad taste. And I can't hide anywhere, for all the world knows me, since I have helped the world.

SHAUVA: Someone's coming!

AZDAK *in a panic walks trembling to the seat:* The game is up! But I'll give no man the pleasure of seeing human greatness. I'll beg on my knees for mercy. Spittle will slobber down my chin. The fear of death is upon me.

Enter Natella Abashvili, the Governor's wife, followed by the Adjutant and an Ironshirt.

THE GOVERNOR'S WIFE: What kind of man is that, Shalva?

AZDAK: A willing one, Your Excellency, a man ready to oblige.

THE ADJUTANT: Natella Abashvili, wife of the late Governor, has just returned and is looking for her three-year-old son, Michael. She has been informed that the child was abducted to the mountains by a former servant.

AZDAK: It will be brought back, Your Highness, at your service.

THE ADJUTANT: They say that the person in question is passing it off as her own child.

AZDAK: She will be beheaded, Your Highness, at your service.

THE ADJUTANT: That's all.

THE GOVERNOR'S WIFE *leaving:* I don't like that man.

AZDAK *following her to the door, and bowing:* Everything will be arranged, Your Highness, at your service.

6

THE CHALK CIRCLE

THE SINGER

Now listen to the story of the trial concerning the child of the Governor Abashvili

To establish the true mother

By the famous test of the Chalk Circle.

The courtyard of the lawcourts in Nukha. Ironshirts lead Michael in, then go across the stage and out at the back. One Ironshirt holds Grusha back under the doorway with his lance until the child has been taken away. Then she is admitted. She is accompanied by the former Governor's cook. Distant noises and a fire-red sky.

GRUSHA: He's so good, he can wash himself already.

THE COOK: You're lucky. This is not a real Judge; this is Azdak. He's a drunk and doesn't understand anything. And the biggest thieves have been acquitted by him, because he mixes everything up and because the rich never offer him big enough bribes. The likes of us get off lightly sometimes.

GRUSHA: I need some luck today.

THE COOK: Touch wood. *She crosses herself.* I think I'd better say a quick prayer that the Judge will be drunk.

Her lips move in prayer, while Grusha looks round in vain for the child.

THE COOK: What I can't understand is why you want to hold on to it at any price, if it's not yours. In these days.

GRUSHA: It's mine, I've brought it up.

THE COOK: But didn't you ever wonder what would happen when she returned?

GRUSHA: At first I thought I'd give it back to her. Then I thought she wouldn't return.

THE COOK: And a borrowed coat keeps one warm, too, eh? *Grusha nods.* I'll swear anything you like, because you're a decent person. *Memorizes aloud:* I had him in my care for five piastres, and on Thursday evening, when the riots started, Grusha came to fetch him. *She sees the soldier, Chachava, approaching.* But you have done Simon great wrong. I've talked to him. He can't understand it.

GRUSHA *unaware of Simon's presence:* I can't be bothered with that man just now, if he doesn't understand anything.

THE COOK: He has understood that the child is not yours; but that you're married and won't be free until death parts you —he can't understand that.

Grusha sees Simon and greets him.

SIMON *gloomily:* I wanted to tell the woman that I am ready to swear I am the father of the child.

GRUSHA *low:* That's right, Simon.

SIMON: At the same time, I would like to say that I am hereby not bound to anything; nor the woman, either.

THE COOK: That's unnecessary. She's married. You know that.

SIMON: That's her business and doesn't need rubbing in.

Enter two Ironshirts.

THE IRONSHIRTS: Where's the Judge?—Has anyone seen the Judge?

GRUSHA *who has turned away and covered her face:* Stand in front of me. I shouldn't have come to Nukha. If I run into the Ironshirt, the one I hit over the head . . .

The Ironshirt who has brought in the child steps forward.

THE IRONSHIRT: The Judge isn't here.

The two Ironshirts go on searching.

THE COOK: I hope something hasn't happened to him. With any other Judge you'd have less chance than a chicken has teeth.

Enter another Ironshirt.

THE IRONSHIRT *who had inquired for the Judge, to the other Ironshirt:* There are only two old people and a child here. The Judge has bolted.

THE OTHER IRONSHIRT: Go on searching!

The first two Ironshirts exit quickly. The third remains behind. Grusha lets out a scream. The Ironshirt turns round. He is the Corporal, and has a large scar right across his face.

THE IRONSHIRT *in the gateway:* What's the matter, Shotta? Do you know her?

THE CORPORAL *after a long stare:* No.

THE IRONSHIRT: She's the one who's supposed to have stolen the Abashvili child. If you know anything about it, Shotta, you can make a packet of money.

Exit the Corporal, cursing.

THE COOK: Was it him? *Grusha nods.* I think he'll keep his mouth shut, otherwise he'll have to admit he was after the child.

GRUSHA *relieved:* I'd almost forgotten I'd saved the child from them . . .

Enter the Governor's wife, followed by the Adjutant and two lawyers.

THE GOVERNOR'S WIFE: Thank God! At least the common people aren't here. I can't stand their smell, it always gives me migraine.

THE FIRST LAWYER: Madam, I must ask you to be as careful as possible in everything you say, until we have another Judge.

THE GOVERNOR'S WIFE: But I didn't say anything, Illo Shuboladze. I love the people—with their simple, straightforward ways. It's just their smell that brings on my migraine.

THE SECOND LAWYER: There will hardly be any spectators. Most of the population is behind locked doors because of the riots in the outer town.

THE GOVERNOR'S WIFE *looking at Grusha:* Is that the creature?

THE FIRST LAWYER: I beg you, most gracious Natella

Abashvili, to abstain from all invective until it is absolutely certain that the Grand Duke has appointed a new Judge and we have got rid of the present one, who is about the lowest ever seen in a Judge's robe. And things seem to be on the move, as you will see.

Ironshirts enter the courtyard.

THE COOK: Her Ladyship wouldn't hesitate to pull your hair out if she didn't know that Azdak is for the poor people. He goes by the face.

Two Ironshirts begin by fastening a rope to the pillar. Azdak, in chains, is led in, followed by Shauva, also in chains. The three farmers bring up the rear.

ONE IRONSHIRT: Trying to run away, eh? *He beats Azdak.*

ONE FARMER: Pull the Judge's robe off before we string him up!

Ironshirts and farmers pull the robe off Azdak. His torn underwear becomes visible. Then someone kicks him.

AN IRONSHIRT *pushing him on to someone else:* Anyone want a bundle of Justice? Here it is!

Accompanied by shouts of 'It's all yours!' and 'I don't want it!' they hurl Azdak back and forth until he collapses. Then he is hauled up and dragged under the noose.

THE GOVERNOR'S WIFE *who, during the 'ball-game', has been clapping her hands hysterically:* I disliked that man from the moment I first saw him.

AZDAK *covered in blood, panting:* I can't see. Give me a rag.

THE OTHER IRONSHIRT: What is it you want to see?

AZDAK: You, you dogs! *He wipes the blood out of his eyes with his shirt.* Good morning, dogs! How are you, dogs? How's the dog world? Does it stink good? Have you got another boot to lick? Are you back at each other's throats, dogs?

Enter a dust-covered rider accompanied by a corporal. He takes some documents from a leather case and looks through them. He interrupts.

THE RIDER: Stop! I bring a despatch from the Grand Duke, containing the latest appointments.

THE CORPORAL *bellows:* Atten - shun!

All jump to attention.

THE RIDER: Of the new Judge it says: We appoint a man whom we have to thank for the saving of a life of the utmost importance to the country. A certain Azdak in Nukha. Which is he?

SHAUVA *pointing:* That's him on the gallows, Your Excellency.

THE CORPORAL *bellowing:* What's going on here?

THE IRONSHIRT: I ask to be allowed to report that His Worship has already been His Worship. He was declared the enemy of the Grand Duke only on these farmers' denunciation.

THE CORPORAL *pointing at the farmers:* March them off! *They are marched off, bowing incessantly.* See to it that His Worship is exposed to no more indignities.

Exit the rider with the corporal.

THE COOK *to Shauva:* She clapped her hands! I hope he saw it!

THE FIRST LAWYER: This is a catastrophe.

Azdak has fainted. Coming to, he is dressed again in a Judge's robe. He walks away, swaying, from the group of Ironshirts.

THE IRONSHIRTS: Don't take it amiss, Your Worship. What are Your Worship's wishes?

AZDAK: Nothing, fellow dogs. An occasional boot to lick. *To Shauva:* I pardon you. *He is unchained.* Fetch me some of the red wine. The sweetest. *Exit Shauva.* Get out of here, I've got to judge a case. *The Ironshirts go. Shauva returns with a jug of wine. Azdak takes deep gulps.* Get me something for my backside. *Shauva brings the Statute Book and puts it on the Judge's seat. Azdak sits on it.* I receive! *The faces of the prosecutors, among whom a worried council has been held, show smiles of relief. They whisper.*

THE COOK: Oh dear!

SIMON: 'A well can't be filled with dew!' they say.

THE LAWYERS *approaching Azdak, who stands up expectantly:* An absolutely ridiculous case, Your Worship. The accused has abducted the child and refuses to hand it over.

AZDAK *stretching out his hand, and glancing at Grusha:* A most attractive person. *He receives more money.* I open the proceedings and demand the absolute truth. *To Grusha:* Especially from you.

THE FIRST LAWYER: High Court of Justice! Blood, as the saying goes, is thicker than water. This old proverb . . .

AZDAK: The Court wants to know the lawyer's fee.

THE FIRST LAWYER *surprised:* I beg your pardon? *Azdak rubs his thumb and index finger.* Oh, I see. 500 piastres, Your Worship, is the answer to the Court's somewhat unusual question.

AZDAK: Did you hear? The question is unusual. I ask it because I listen to you in a quite different way if I know you are good.

THE FIRST LAWYER *bowing:* Thank you, Your Worship. High Court of Justice! Of all bonds the bonds of blood are the strongest. Mother and child—is there a more intimate relationship? Can one tear a child from its mother? High Court of Justice! She has conceived it in the holy ecstasies of love. She has carried it in her womb. She has fed it with her blood. She has borne it with pain. High Court of Justice! It has been observed, Your Worship, how even the wild tigress, robbed of her young, roams restless through the mountains, reduced to a shadow. Nature herself . . .

AZDAK *interrupting, to Grusha:* What's your answer to all this and anything else the lawyer might have to say?

GRUSHA: He's mine.

AZDAK: Is that all? I hope you can prove it. In any case, I advise you to tell me why you think the child should be given to you.

GRUSHA: I've brought him up according to my best knowledge and conscience. I always found him something to eat. Most of the time he had a roof over his head. And I went to all sorts of trouble for him. I had expenses, too. I didn't think of my own comfort. I brought up the child to be friendly with everyone. And from the beginning I taught him to work as well as he could. But he's still very small.

THE FIRST LAWYER: Your Worship, it is significant that the person herself doesn't claim any bond of blood between herself and this child.

AZDAK: The Court takes note.

THE FIRST LAWYER: Thank you, Your Worship. Please permit a woman who has suffered much—who has already lost her husband and now also has to fear the loss of her child—to address a few words to you. Her Highness, Natella Abashvili . . .

THE GOVERNOR'S WIFE *quietly:* A most cruel fate, sir, forces me to ask you to return my beloved child. It's not for me to describe to you the tortures of a bereaved mother's soul, the anxiety, the sleepless nights, the . . .

THE SECOND LAWYER *exploding:* It's outrageous the way this woman is treated. She's not allowed to enter her husband's palace. The revenue of her estates is blocked. She is told cold-bloodedly that it's tied to the heir. She can't do anything without the child. She can't even pay her lawyers. *To the first lawyer who, desperate about this outburst, makes frantic gestures to stop him speaking:* Dear Illo Shuboladze, why shouldn't it be divulged now that it's the Abashvili estates that are at stake?

THE FIRST LAWYER: Please, Honoured Sandro Oboladze! We had agreed . . . *To Azdak:* Of course it is correct that the trial will also decide whether our noble client will obtain the right to dispose of the large Abashvili estates. I say 'also' on purpose, because in the foreground stands the human tragedy of a mother, as Natella Abashvili has rightly explained at the beginning of her moving statement. Even if Michael Abashvili were *not* the heir to the estates, he would still be the dearly beloved child of my client.

AZDAK: Stop! The Court is touched by the mention of the estates. It's a proof of human feeling.

THE SECOND LAWYER: Thanks, Your Worship. Dear Illo Shuboladze, in any case we can prove that the person who

took possession of the child is not the child's mother.
Permit me to lay before the Court the bare facts. By an unfortunate chain of circumstances, the child, Michael Abashvili, was left behind while his mother was making her
escape. Grusha, the Palace kitchenmaid, was present on this
Easter Sunday and was observed busying herself with the
child . . .

THE COOK: All her mistress was thinking about was what
kind of dresses she would take along.

THE SECOND LAWYER *unmoved:* Almost a year later Grusha
turned up in a mountain village with a child, and there
entered into matrimony with . . .

AZDAK: How did you get into that mountain village?

GRUSHA: On foot, Your Worship. And he was mine.

SIMON: I am the father, Your Worship.

THE COOK: I had him in my care for five piastres, Your
Worship.

THE SECOND LAWYER: This man is engaged to Grusha,
High Court of Justice, and for this reason his testimony is
not reliable.

AZDAK: Are you the man she married in the mountain
village?

SIMON: No, Your Worship, she married a peasant.

AZDAK *winking at Grusha:* Why? *Pointing at Simon:* Isn't he
any good in bed? Tell the truth.

GRUSHA: We didn't get that far. I married because of the
child, so that he should have a roof over his head. *Pointing
at Simon.* He was in the war, Your Worship.

AZDAK: And now he wants you again, eh?

SIMON: I want to state in evidence . . .

GRUSHA *angrily:* I am no longer free, Your Worship.

AZDAK: And the child, you claim, is the result of whoring?
Grusha does not answer. I'm going to ask you a question:
What kind of child is it? Is it one of those ragged street-
urchins? Or is it a child from a well-to-do family?

GRUSHA *angrily:* It's an ordinary child.

AZDAK: I mean, did he have fine features from the beginning?

GRUSHA: He had a nose in his face.

AZDAK: He had a nose in his face. I consider that answer of yours to be important. They say of me that once, before passing judgment, I went out and sniffed at a rosebush. Tricks of this kind are necessary nowadays. I'll cut things short now, and listen no longer to your lies. *To Grusha:* Especially yours. *To the group of defendants:* I can imagine what you've cooked up between you to cheat me. I know you. You're swindlers.

GRUSHA *suddenly:* I can quite understand your wanting to cut it short, having seen what you received!

AZDAK: Shut up! Did I receive anything from you?

GRUSHA *while the cook tries to restrain her:* Because I haven't got anything.

AZDAK: Quite true. I never get a thing from starvelings. I might just as well starve myself. You want justice, but do you want to pay for it? When you go to the butcher you know you have to pay. But to the Judge you go as though to a funeral supper.

SIMON *loudly:* 'When the horse was shod, the horsefly stretched out its leg', as the saying is.

AZDAK *eagerly accepting the challenge:* 'Better a treasure in the sewer than a stone in the mountain stream.'

SIMON: ' "A fine day. Let's go fishing," said the angler to the worm.'

AZDAK: ' "I'm my own master," said the servant, and cut off his foot.'

SIMON: ' "I love you like a father," said the Czar to the peasant, and had the Czarevitch's head chopped off.'

AZDAK: 'The fool's worst enemy is himself.'

SIMON: But 'a fart has no nose'.

AZDAK: Fined ten piastres for indecent language in Court. That'll teach you what Justice is.

GRUSHA: That's a fine kind of Justice. You jump on us because we don't talk so refined as that lot with their lawyers.

AZDAK: Exactly. The likes of you are too stupid. It's only right that you should get it in the neck.

GRUSHA: Because you want to pass the child on to her. She who is too refined even to know how to change its nappies! You don't know any more about Justice than I do, that's clear.

AZDAK: There's something in that. I'm an ignorant man. I haven't even a decent pair of trousers under my robe. See for yourself. With me, everything goes on food and drink. I was educated in a convent school. Come to think of it, I'll fine you ten piastres, too. For contempt of Court. What's more, you're a very silly girl to turn me against you, instead of making eyes at me and wagging your backside a bit to keep me in a good temper. Twenty piastres!

GRUSHA: Even if it were thirty, I'd tell you what I think of your justice, you drunken onion! How dare you talk to me as though you were the cracked Isaiah on the church window! When they pulled you out of your mother, it wasn't planned that you'd rap her over the knuckles for pinching a little bowl of corn from somewhere! Aren't you ashamed of yourself when you see how afraid I am of you? But you've let yourself become their servant. So that their houses are not taken away, because they've stolen them. Since when do houses belong to bed-bugs? But you're on the look-out, otherwise they couldn't drag our men into their wars. You bribe-taker!

Azdak gets up. He begins to beam. With a little hammer he knocks on the table half-heartedly as if to get silence. But as Grusha's scolding continues, he only beats time with it.

I've no respect for you. No more than for a thief or a murderer with a knife, who does what he wants. You can take the child away from me, a hundred against one, but I tell you one thing: for a profession like yours, they ought to choose only bloodsuckers and men who rape children. As a punishment. To make them sit in judgment over their fellow men, which is worse than swinging from the gallows.

AZDAK *sitting down:* Now it will be thirty! And I won't go on brawling with you as though we were in a tavern. What would happen to my dignity as a Judge? I've lost all interest in your case. Where's the couple who wanted a divorce? *To Shauva:* Bring them in. This case is adjourned for fifteen minutes.

THE FIRST LAWYER *to the Governor's wife:* Without producing any more evidence, Madam, we have the verdict in the bag.

THE COOK *to Grusha:* You've gone and spoiled your chances with him. You won't get the child now.

Enter a very old couple.

THE GOVERNOR'S WIFE: Shalva, my smelling salts!

AZDAK: I receive. *The old couple do not understand.* I hear you want to be divorced. How long have you been living together?

THE OLD WOMAN: Forty years, Your Worship.

AZDAK: And why d'you want a divorce?

THE OLD MAN: We don't like each other, Your Worship.

AZDAK: Since when?

THE OLD WOMAN: Oh, from the very beginning, Your Worship.

AZDAK: I'll consider your case and deliver my verdict when I'm finished with the other one. *Shauva leads them into the background.* I need the child. *He beckons Grusha towards him and bends not unkindly towards her.* I've noticed that you have a soft spot for justice. I don't believe he's your child, but if he were yours, woman, wouldn't you want him to be rich? You'd only have to say he isn't yours and at once he'd have a palace, scores of horses in his stable, scores of beggars on his doorstep, scores of soldiers in his service, and scores of petitioners in his courtyard. Now, what d'you say? Don't you want him to be rich?

Grusha is silent.

THE SINGER: Listen now to what the angry girl thought, but didn't say. *He sings:*

He who wears the shoes of gold
Tramples on the weak and old
Does evil all day long
And mocks at wrong.

O to carry as one's own
Heavy is the heart of stone.
The power to do ill
Wears out the will.

Hunger he will dread
Not those who go unfed:
Fear the fall of night
But not the light.

AZDAK: I think I understand you, woman.

GRUSHA: I won't give him away. I've brought him up, and he knows me.

Enter Shauva with the child.

THE GOVERNOR'S WIFE: It's in rags!

GRUSHA: That's not true. I wasn't given the time to put on his good shirt.

THE GOVERNOR'S WIFE: It's been in a pig-sty.

GRUSHA *furious:* I'm no pig, but there are others who are. Where did you leave your child?

THE GOVERNOR'S WIFE: I'll let you have it, you vulgar person. *She is about to throw herself on Grusha, but is restrained by her lawyers.* She's a criminal! She must be flogged! Right away!

THE SECOND LAWYER *holding his hand over her mouth:* Most gracious Natella Abashvili, you promised . . . Your Worship, the plaintiff's nerves . . .

AZDAK: Plaintiff and defendant! The Court has listened to your case, and has come to no decision as to who the real mother of this child is. I as Judge have the duty of choosing a mother for the child. I'll make a test. Shauva, get a piece of chalk and draw a circle on the floor. *Shauva does so.* Now place the child in the centre. *Shauva puts Michael, who smiles at Grusha, in the centre of the circle.* Plaintiff and defendant, stand near the circle, both of you. *The Governor's wife and Grusha step up to the circle.* Now each of you take the child by a hand. The true mother is she who has the strength to pull the child out of the circle, towards herself.

THE SECOND LAWYER *quickly:* High Court of Justice, I protest! I object that the fate of the great Abashvili estates, which are bound up with the child as the heir, should be made dependent on such a doubtful wrestling match. Moreover, my client does not command the same physical strength as this person, who is accustomed to physical work.

AZDAK: She looks pretty well fed to me. Pull!

The Governor's wife pulls the child out of the circle to her side. Grusha has let it go and stands aghast.

THE FIRST LAWYER *congratulating the Governor's wife:* What did I say! The bonds of blood!

AZDAK *to Grusha:* What's the matter with you? You didn't pull!

GRUSHA: I didn't hold on to him. *She runs to Azdak.* Your Worship, I take back everything I said against you. I ask your forgiveness. If I could just keep him until he can speak properly. He knows only a few words.

AZDAK: Don't influence the Court! I bet you know only twenty yourself. All right, I'll do the test once more, to make certain.

The two women take up positions again.

AZDAK: Pull!

Again Grusha lets go of the child.

GRUSHA *in despair:* I've brought him up! Am I to tear him to pieces? I can't do it!

AZDAK *rising:* And in this manner the Court has established the true mother. *To Grusha:* Take your child and be off with it. I advise you not to stay in town with him. *To the Governor's wife:* And you disappear before I fine you for fraud. Your estates fall to the city. A playground for children will be made out of them. They need one, and I have decided it shall be called after me—The Garden of Azdak.

The Governor's wife has fainted and is carried out by the Adjutant. Her lawyers have preceded her. Grusha stands motionless. Shauwa leads the child towards her.

AZDAK: Now I'll take off this Judge's robe—it has become

too hot for me. I'm not cut out for a hero. But I invite you all to a little farewell dance, outside on the meadow. Oh, I had almost forgotten something in my excitement. I haven't signed the decree for divorce.

Using the Judge's seat as a table, he writes something on a piece of paper and prepares to leave. Dance music has started.

SHAUVA *having read what is on the paper:* But that's not right. You haven't divorced the old couple. You've divorced Grusha from her husband.

AZDAK: Have I divorced the wrong ones? I'm sorry, but it'll have to stand. I never retract anything. If I did, there'd be no law and order. *To the old couple:* Instead, I'll invite you to my feast. You won't mind dancing with each other. *To Grusha and Simon:* I've still got 40 piastres coming from you.

SIMON *pulling out his purse:* That's cheap, Your Worship. And many thanks.

AZDAK *pocketing the money:* I'll need it.

GRUSHA: So we'd better leave town tonight, eh, Michael? *About to take the child on her back. To Simon:* You like him?

SIMON *taking the child on his back:* With my respects, I like him.

GRUSHA: And now I can tell you: I took him because on that Easter Sunday I got engaged to you. And so it is a child of love. Michael, let's dance.

She dances with Michael. Simon dances with the cook. The old couple dance with each other. Azdak stands lost in thought. The dancers soon hide him from view. Occasionally he is seen again, but less and less as more couples enter and join the dance.

THE SINGER

And after this evening Azdak disappeared and was never seen again.

But the people of Grusinia did not forget him and often remembered

His time of Judgment as a brief

Golden Age that was almost just.

The dancing couples dance out. Azdak has disappeared.

But you, who have listened to the story of the Chalk
   Circle
Take note of the meaning of the ancient song:
That what there is shall belong to those who are good for
   it, thus
The children to the maternal, that they thrive;
The carriages to good drivers, that they are driven well;
And the valley to the waterers, that it shall bear fruit.

THE CAUCASIAN CHALK CIRCLE

Texts by Brecht

NOTES TO THE CAUCASIAN CHALK CIRCLE

1. *Realism and stylization*

Actors, stage designers and directors normally achieve stylization at the cost of realism. They create a style by creating 'the' peasant, 'the' wedding, 'the' battlefield; in other words by removing whatever is unique, special, contradictory, accidental, and providing hackneyed or hackneyable stereotypes the bulk of which represent no mastery of reality but are just drawings of drawings—simple to provide since the originals already have elements of style in them. Such stylists have no style of their own, nor any wish to grasp that of reality; all they do is to imitate methods of stylization. Plainly all art embellishes (which is not the same as glossing over). If for no other reason it must do so because it has to link reality with enjoyment. But this kind of embellishment, formulation, stylization, must not involve phoneyness or loss of substance. Any actress who plays *Grusha* needs to study the beauty of Brueghel's 'Dulle Griet'.

2. *Tension*

The play was written in America after ten years of exile, and its structure is partly conditioned by a revulsion against the commercialized dramaturgy of Broadway. At the same time it makes use of certain elements of that older American theatre whose forte lay in burlesques and 'shows'. In those highly imaginative manifestations, which recall the films of that splendid man Chaplin, the tension focused not merely on the progress of the plot (or only in a much cruder and larger sense than now), but more on the question 'How?'

Nowadays when we are 'offered an amusing trifle' it is simply the feverish efforts of a rapidly ageing whore who hopes that her graceless tricks will serve to postpone or annul the moment when her painful and frequently-operated vagina has once again to be handed over to a client. The pleasure of telling a story is inhibited by fear that it will fall flat. Unleashing this pleasure however does not mean freeing it from all control. Detail will be of the greatest importance, but that does not mean that economy won't be of great importance too. Imagination can be applied to the achievement of brevity. The point is not to abandon something rich. The worst enemy of true playing is playing about; meandering is the sign of a bad story-teller, while cosiness is just self-satisfaction and to be despised as such. Direct statement is among the most important methods of epic art, and it is as fair to [speak] of epic restlessness as of epic repose.

3. The chalk circle

The test of the chalk circle in the old Chinese novel and play, like their biblical counterpart, Solomon's test of the sword, still remain valuable tests of motherhood (by establishing motherliness) even if motherhood today has to be socially rather than biologically defined. The 'Caucasian Chalk Circle' is not a parable. Possibly the prologue may create confusion on this point, since it looks superficially as if the whole story is being told in order to clear up the argument about who owns the valley. On closer inspection however the story is seen to be a true narrative which of itself proves nothing but merely displays a particular kind of wisdom, a potentially model attitude for the argument in question. Seen this way, the prologue becomes a background which situates the practicability and also the evolution of such wisdom in an historic setting. And so the theatre must not use the kind of technique developed by it for plays of the parable type.

4. Background and foreground

In the English language there is an American term 'sucker',

and this is exactly what Grusha is being when she takes over the child. The Austrian term 'die Wurzen' means something of the same sort, while in High German one would have to say 'der Dumme', 'the fool' (as in the context 'they've managed to find somebody fool enough to . . .'). Her maternal instincts lay Grusha open to troubles and tribulations which prove very nearly fatal. All she wants of Azdak is permission to go on producing, in other words to pay more. She loves the child; her claim to it is based on the fact that she is willing and able to be productive. She is no longer a sucker after the hearing.

5. [Setting of the play]
The play's setting needs to be very simple. The varying backgrounds can be indicated by some form of projection; at the same time the projections must be artistically valid. The bit players can in some cases play several parts at once. The five musicians sit on stage with the singer and join in the action.

6. Incidental music for the Chalk Circle
Aside from certain songs which can take personal expression, the story-teller's music need only display a cold beauty, but it should not be unduly difficult. Though I think it is possible to make particularly effective use of a certain kind of monotony, the musical basis of the five acts needs to be clearly varied. The opening song of Act 1 should have something barbaric about it, and the underlying rhythm be a preparation and accompaniment for the entry of the governor's family and the soldiers beating back the crowd. The mimed song at the end of the act should be cold, so that the girl Grusha can play against the grain of it.

For Act 2 ('The Flight into the northern mountains') the theatre calls for thrustful music to hold this extremely epic act together; none the less it must be thin and delicate.

Act 3 has the melting snow music (poetical) and, for its main scene, funeral and wedding music in contrast with one another. The song in the scene by the river has the same theme as the Act 1 song in which Grusha promises the soldier to wait for him.

In act 4 the thrustful, scurrilous Ballad of Azdak must be interrupted twice by Azdak's two songs (which definitely have to be simple to sing, since Azdak must be played by the most powerful actor rather than by the best singer). The last (lawsuit) act demands a good dance at the end.

7. Behaviour of the Singer in the last scene of Act 1

The playwright suggested that the general principle of having the scenes embody specific passages of the singer's song in such a way that their performance never overshadows the singer's solo performance to the villagers ought to be deliberately abandoned in production.

8. Casting of Azdak

It is essential to have an actor who can portray an utterly upright man. Azdak is utterly upright, a disappointed revolutionary posing as a human wreck, like Shakespeare's wise men who act the fool. Without this the judgement of the chalk circle would lose all its authority.

9. Palace revolution

The curt orders given offstage inside the palace (sporadically and in some cases quietly so as to imply the palace's vast size) must be cut once they have served to help the actors at rehearsal. What is going on onstage is not supposed to be a slice of some larger occurrence, just the part of it to be seen at this precise spot outside the palace gate. It is the entire occurrence, and the gate is *the* gate. (Nor is the size of the palace to be conveyed in spatial terms.) What we have to do is replace our extras with good actors. One good actor is worth a whole battalion of extras; i.e. he is more.

[Sections 1–6, 8, and 9 are from GW *Schriften zum Theater 17*, pp. 1204–8. The typescripts suggest that 1–4 belong together, and we have put them in their original,

possibly accidental but still logical order. They and
section 6 are thought to date from 1944. Sections 5 and 7
are notes accompanying the first version of the script
that year, 7 being taken from BBA 192/178. The last two
were written nearly ten years later, 8 being assigned to
about 1953 by BBA while 9 relates to a rehearsal held on
4 December of that year in preparation for Brecht's Ber-
liner Ensemble production.]

DANCE OF THE GRAND DUKE WITH HIS BOW

Oh, the green fields of Samara!
Oh, the bent backs of a warlike race!
O sun, o domination!

I am your prince. This bow they are bringing
Is elm tipped with bronze, strung with flexible sinew.
This arrow is mine, which I mean to send winging
To plunge itself deep, O my enemy, in you.

Oh, the green fields of Samara!
Oh, the bent backs of a warlike race!
O sun, o domination!

Off, off to the fight, bowstring taut. Aren't you frightened
To feel how much deeper the bronze will go worming
Its way through your flesh as the bowstring is tightened?
Fly, arrow, and cut up that enemy vermin!

So I tug, tug and tug at the bow that they made me.
How strong are my shoulders! A fraction more. Steady . . .
Why, it's broken! All lies! Elm and bronze have betrayed me.
Help, Help! God have mercy: my soul's so unready.

Oh, the cattle-stocked fields of Samara!
Oh, the bent backs of a warlike race!
Oh, the cutting up of the enemy!

[BBA 28/23-4. A pencilled note by Elisabeth Hauptmann, dating probably from the 1950s or later, identifies
this as material discarded from the play.]

CONCERNING THE PROLOGUE

Your dislike of the prologue puzzles me somewhat; it was the first bit of the play to be written by me in the States. You see, the problem posed by this parable-like play has got to be derived from real-life needs, and in my view this was achieved in a light and cheerful manner. Take away the prologue, and it becomes impossible to understand on the one hand why it wasn't left as the Chinese Chalk Circle, and on the other why it should be called Caucasian. I first of all wrote the little story which was published in *Tales from the Calendar*. But on coming to dramatize it I felt just this lack of elucidatory historical background.

> [From Werner Hecht (ed.): *Materialien zu Brecht's 'Der kaukasische Kreidekreis'*, Suhrkamp-Verlag, Frankfurt, 1966, p. 28. This passage is taken from a letter to Brecht's publisher Peter Suhrkamp, and reflects a common attitude among West German critics and theatre directors. The 'little story' was 'The Augsburg Chalk Circle', for which see p. 313.]

CONTRADICTIONS IN 'THE CAUCASIAN CHALK CIRCLE'

1. Main contradictions

The more Grusha does to save the child's life, the more she endangers her own; her productivity tends to her own destruction. That is how things are, given the conditions of war, the law as it is, and her isolation and poverty. In the law's eyes the rescuer is a thief. Her poverty is a threat to the child, and the child adds to it. For the child's sake she needs a husband, but she is in danger of losing one on its account. And so forth.

Bit by bit, by making sacrifices, not least of herself, Grusha becomes transformed into a mother for the child; and finally, having risked or suffered so many losses, fears no loss more than that of the child. Azdak's judgment makes the rescue of the child absolute. He is free to award the child to her because there is no longer any difference between the child's interests and hers.

Azdak is the disappointed man who is not going to cause disappointment in others.

2. Other contradictions

The petitioners prostrate themselves before the governor as he goes to Easter Mass. Beaten back by the Ironshirts, they fight wildly among themselves for a place in the front row.

The same peasant who overcharges Grusha for his milk is then kindly enough to help her pick up the child. He isn't mean; he's poor.

The architects make utterly servile obeisances to the governor's ADC, but one of them has to watch the other two to see how they do it. They are not just natural arse-creepers; they need the job.

Grusha's spineless brother is reluctant to take in his sister, but furious with his kulak of a wife on account of his dependence on her.

This spineless brother cannot say boo to his kulak of a wife, but is overbearing to the peasant woman with whom he fixes up the marriage contract.

The motherly instincts of the peasant woman who takes in the foundling against her husband's wishes are limited and provisional; she betrays it to the police. (Likewise Grusha's motherly instincts, though they are so much greater, so very great, are limited and provisional: she wants to see the child into safety, then give it away.)

The maid Grusha is against war because it has torn her beloved from her; she recommends him always to stay in the middle in order to survive. However on her flight into the mountains she sings of the popular hero Sosso Robakidse who conquered Iran, in order to keep her courage up.

[GW *Schriften zum Theater 17*, pp. 1208–10. Assigned by BBA to 1954. However, Brecht's concept of main and subsidiary contradictions (i.e. conflicting elements in a situation) derives from Mao Tse-tung, whose pamphlet *On Contradiction* he seems to have read in 1955.]

SIDE TRACK

P: The people at X want to cut 'the flight into the northern mountains'. The play is a long one, and they argue that this whole act is really no more than a side track. One sees how the maid wants to get rid of the child as soon as she has got it away from the immediate danger zone; but then she keeps it after all, and that, they say, is what counts.

B: Side tracks in modern plays have to be studied carefully before one makes up one's mind to take a short cut. It might turn out to seem longer. Certain theatres cut one of Macheath's two arrests in the *Threepenny Opera* on the grounds that both might have occurred because he twice went to the brothel instead of clearing out. They made him come to grief because he went to the brothel, not because he went to it too often, was careless. In short they hoped to liven things up and finished by getting tedious.

P: They say it weakens the maid's claim to the child in the trial scene if her feeling for him is shown as subject to limitations.

B: To start with, the trial scene isn't about the maid's claim to the child but about the child's claim to the better mother. And the maid's suitability for being a mother, her usefulness and reliability are shown precisely by her level-headed reservations about taking the child on.

R: Even her reservations strike me as beautiful. Friendliness is not unlimited, it is subject to measure. A person has just so much friendliness—no more, no less—and it is furthermore dependent on the situation at the time. It can be exhausted, can be replenished, and so on and so forth.

W: I'd call that a realistic view.

B: It's too mechanical a one for me: unfriendly. Why not look at it this way? Evil times make humane feelings a danger to humanity. Inside the maid Grusha the child's interests and her own are at loggerheads with one another. She must acknowledge both interests and do her best to promote them both. This way of looking at it, I think, must lead to a richer and more flexible portrayal of the Grusha part. It's true.

[From 'Die Dialektik auf dem Theater' in *Versuche 15*, Suhrkamp and Aufbau Verlags, 1956. As with other dialogues in that collection, Brecht shows himself as B, talking with some of his young collaborators: in this case P for Peter Palitzsch, R for Kathe Rülicke and W for Manfred Wekwerth. They were not literal transcriptions.]

Editorial Note

The Caucasian Chalk Circle brings together two threads that had been twining their way gently through Brecht's mind for several years before Luise Rainer asked him to write the play. They are of course the old Chinese story of the chalk circle, with its strong resemblance to the Judgement of Solomon, and the story of the eccentric, paradoxical judge which (though one can never be certain of this) Brecht appears to have devised for himself. Of the two the former probably has the longer ancestry—in Brecht's mind, that is—for Klabund's modern German dramatization was staged by Max Reinhardt at the Deutsches Theater, where Brecht had just spent a year as a junior dramaturg, on 20 October 1925. Brecht knew Klabund, or Alfred Henschke (as he was really called), from Munich as a writer and singer of ballads faintly akin to his own—he had actually replaced Brecht in the second performance of the *Red Raisin* programme that followed *Drums in the Night* there—and Klabund's wife the actress Carola Neher was to become one of Brecht's best-loved performers. Moreover his still earlier friend, her unrelated namesake Caspar Neher, was designer for the new play, while Elisabeth Bergner, then coming to the peak of her fame in Germany, played its leading part. 'We all saw it,' said Hanns Eisler later.

Described as '*The Chalk Circle*. A play in five acts from the Chinese, by Klabund', the text was published the same year (by J. M. Spaeth Verlag, Berlin). In fact it and its heroine the prostitute Haitang have a good deal more in common with *The Good Person of Szechwan* than with *The Caucasian Chalk Circle*, and almost certainly helped also to inspire the former play, which was already written by the time of Brecht's arrival in the U.S. Even the basic situation of the chalk circle differs from Brecht's version, in that the heroine (who naturally wins the test) is the biological mother and the false claimant a stepmother, while the symbolism of the circle is already underlined by Haitang and her princely lover in the first Act, as he draws one in white on a black wall, to represent the vaulted sky and the uniting of two hearts:

HAITANG: Whatever lies outside this circle is nothing. Whatever lies inside this circle is everything. How are everything and nothing linked? In the circle that turns and moves (*drawing spokes in the circle*)—in the wheel that rolls . . .

The test is conducted twice, first by the corrupt judge Tschu-tschu in Act 3, when Haitang loses, then again by her old lover, now become emperor, in Act 5. 'Take a piece of chalk', says the emperor to his master of ceremonies:

> draw a circle here on the ground before my throne, put the boy in the circle.
>
> MASTER OF CEREMONIES: It has been done.
>
> EMPEROR: And now, both you women,
> Try to draw the boy out of the circle
> At the same time. One of you take his left arm,
> The other his right. It is certain
> The right mother will have the right strength
> To draw the boy out of the circle to herself.
>
> *The women do as he says. Haitang grips the boy gently; Mrs Ma tugs him brutally to her side.* It is clear that this person *indicating Haitang* cannot be the mother. Otherwise she would have managed to draw the boy out of the circle. Let the women repeat the experiment. *Mrs Ma once again pulls the boy to her side.* Haitang, I see that you do not make the slightest effort to draw the boy out of the circle to you. What's the meaning of that?

Haitang explains that, having brought the child up, she knows that his arms are too delicate to stand tugging:

> If the only way I can get my child is by pulling off his arms, then let somebody who has never known a mother's sufferings for her child pull him out of the circle.
>
> EMPEROR *standing up:* Behold the mighty power locked in the chalk circle! This woman *indicating Mrs Ma* aimed to get control of all Mr Ma's fortune and to that end seized the child. Now that the real mother has been acknowledged it will be possible to find the real murderer . . .

for Mrs Ma had murdered their joint husband and accused Haitang of the crime. She now confesses, and together with the judge is pardoned by Haitang, who is left alone with her son and her imperial lover as the curtain falls.

At the time this slightly sugary play provoked Brecht to parody it, making Jackie Pall in *The Elephant Calf* of 1926 (Vol. 2 of the *Collected Plays*) pull his mother out of a 'doubtless most incompetently drawn circle' in order to prove contrariwise that he, the elephant child, is her son or alternatively her daughter. It also stimulated Friedrich Wolf to write the counterplay *Tai-yang erwacht*, originally to be called *Haitang wakes up*. Roughly twelve years later, however, when Brecht was living in Svendborg, he took up the theme again and must have wondered whether to give it a Chinese or a European setting. The title *The Odense Chalk Circle* (Odense being the principal city of Fünen Island, where Svendborg is situated) seems to suggest the latter, but only a few fragmentary notes under this heading are left, e.g.:

> the governor who has to act like a poor man. he pretends to eat too crudely and is sharply rebuked.

—and:

> the gentry are scared because the governor has been driven out. they flee, fully expecting the peasantry to institute a bloodbath.
>
> but the peasants don't come and there is no bloodbath.
>
> by an oversight the judge appointed by the rebels is confirmed by the governor.
>
> he pronounces judgement in the case of the two mothers.

There was to be a character called Hieronymus Dan, while another note suggests accompaniment by 'old and austere music (fifes, drums, organs)'. There is also however a more coherent scheme headed simply *The Chalk Circle*, and this is full of Chinese names. It appears to go thus:

I

> how schao-fan gets to be a judge. he hides a hunted man. this upsets his wedding. the bride's family withdraws.
>
> the peasants propose schao-fan for the judge's post. laughter all round.
>
> the governor returns to power and sends a messenger appointing a judge: schao-fan.
>
> the wedding takes place. ([what] was taken out is brought back in before the scene starts, silently or to a song: love is an irresistible force, etc.) the new judge gives judgement in a long lawsuit between the village and the bride's family. the judge finds for the village by sticking to the letter of the law.

II

the judge's pranks. he gets drunk in a case involving property and makes everything depend on what shape one of the litigants' nose is, etc.

he is put in gaol. his house is destroyed as if by a tornado.

the maid's wanderings with the child. through the dangers of the blizzard, through the worse dangers of the slums.

she rejects good food for the child and exposes it to hunger.

III

the mother denies the child. by acknowledging him she would be acknowledging that she is the judge's wife.

the maid adopts it, mutely, behind her own back, like a jack-daw whose thieving is hereditary.

IV

the judge gets his post back by mistake.

he bribes witnesses, he fails to examine them once bribed, he muddles everything, proposes marriage to a lady witness in open court and so on.

Section III was later shifted to precede Section I.

A single sample of the dialogue (BBA 128/05–06) shows how Brecht's interest was already centring on the disreputable judge, and goes on to outline a 'second part' in which the heroine is again called Haitang:

PEOPLE: he's a very bad judge. he breaks the law—no, he's never read it—ay, it was pure accident he got the job. he used to be a rice planter. one night an old man broke into his paddy-fields and begged him to have mercy: soldiers were after him. tao schun was sorry for him and hid him in his hut under some old baskets. that old man was the governor of the province, and after the foiling of the plot against him that night thanks to his flight and the planter's sympathy he quickly smote down his enemies. he had the planter trained and made him a judge. but tao schun was a great disappoint-ment to him. he said quite openly in a bar that it just hadn't occurred to him to ask the old man what level of society he came from. and so he had treated him as a fugitive not as a governor. but for that he'd no doubt have handed him over to the soldiers. he regretted having saved one of the oppressors. —for some time they've only been giving cases to tao schun when the senior judge is ill, like today.

PARTY WAITING *jump up appalled:* is it really tao schun on the bench today? if so we must have an adjournment. *to one another:* he won't accept a thing. we're sunk.

PARTY OPPOSITE: tao schun's in charge! hear that? it's all up, then. he won't accept a thing.

PARTY OF THE FIRST PART: hey, you! we've just been told one of our family's seriously ill. so we'd like to go home. would it make any difference to you if we held the case some other day? *in an undertone:* you dirty lot of vultures!

PARTY OF THE SECOND PART: it's all the same to us so long as the truth comes out.

THE FIRST FAMILY: you're right there. better lose our field tomorrow than today. let's go. *exeunt.*

THE FAMILY OPPOSITE *as they leave:* those crooks. wait till judge tai's recovered, that'll put paid to their claims even if it costs us 50 taels.

THE JUDGE, TAO SCHUN *sings:*
the judge is unwell, his thumb's feeling sore—
he pretends to count money
—so today there's a healthier look to the law.
but what d'you imagine a verdict is for?
eat your fill; then you'll stink all the more.

The few notes headed 'second part' follow:

haitang is caught in the civil war. together with the child, she is forced to take risks for the sake of the cause. she exposes the child to many dangers. their journey through the blizzard. cheerful song. their journey through the slums. (more dangerous.)

L:

in face of a snowstorm
i once was full of courage
but in face of people
i now am cowardly.
the snowstorm will not destroy us.
the earthquake is not avid for us.
but the coal merchant wants money
and the shipowner must be paid for the voyage.

Even before leaving Denmark however Brecht had begun work on *The Good Person of Szechwan*, for which this last 'aria' could easily have been written, and around the same time he seems to have set aside the oriental version of the story and started to see the judge figure in German garb. Thus Mother Courage, in the 1939 script of that play, recalls a corrupt judge in Franconia who sounds very like him (*Collected Plays*, Vol. 5) while the following year Brecht wrote the short story 'The Augsburg Chalk Circle' which appeared in the June 1941 issue of the Moscow *Internationale Literatur* and later in *Tales from the Calendar*. This develops the theme a lot further in the direction of our play, at the same time shifting it bodily to Brecht's own home town and the period of the Thirty Years War. Here the child's mother, fleeing before the invading Catholics, spends too long packing her clothes and runs off without it. Instead Anna the maid takes charge, watching by it much as does Grusha at the end of scene 2:

> When she had spent some time, an hour perhaps, watching how the child breathed and sucked at its little fist, she realized that she had sat too long and seen too much to be able to leave without the child. Clumsily she stood up, wrapped it in its linen coverlet, took it on her arm and went out of the courtyard with it, looking shyly around like someone with a bad conscience, a thief [cf. p. 25].

She takes it off to her brother's in the country; he then makes her marry a dying cottager with the same results as in the eventual play. When the child's mother arrives 'several years' later and removes it she sues for her boy's return. The judge is one Ignaz Dollinger, who is described as 'a short but extremely meaty old man', famous for 'his homely hearings, with their cutting remarks and proverbs' and accordingly 'praised by the lower orders in a lengthy ballad'. 'Is he yours?' he bellows at her, accusing her of being after the dead father's property. 'Yes', she replies, '. . . If I can just keep him till he knows all the words. He only knows seven' (cf. p. 95). So he hears the case, concludes that both mothers are lying, and makes the test of the chalk circle, in which Anna lets the boy go, so that he is jerked to his mother's side.

> Old Dollinger got to his feet.
> 'And that shows us', he announced in a loud voice, 'who the right mother is. Take the child away from that slut. She'd tear him cold-bloodedly in two.'

Three or four years later, when Jules Leventhal commissioned him to write the play for Broadway (which may seem inconsistent with his professed 'revulsion' but was not wholly so), the main structure and principal characters were ready in Brecht's mind, and the only remaining problems were setting and framework: what period and country to pick for it and how to relate it to the present day. The choice of medieval Georgia and of a contemporary Soviet framework must already have been made before he left New York in mid-March 1944 to return to Santa Monica and work on the script, for there is no sign of hesitation. Certainly the resulting first script is written with great sureness and an unusual scarcity of amendments and afterthoughts, while there are far fewer drafts and alternative versions than for some of the less complex or elaborately developed plays. The dating of the framework was to change; in the first script the prologue is set in 1934, without reference to the war. So were most of the names of the characters, which started by being mainly Russian and were Georgianized later; thus Grusha Vachnadze was originally Katya Grusha (or at one point Katya Kirshon), her soldier Volodya Surki, her brother Piotr and the lesser characters Petrov Petrovitch, Maxim Maximovitch and the like, while the princes were Boyars and Grusinia Georgia throughout.

Just when the various alterations were made is impossible to say. A journal entry of 8 May shows that Brecht was held up for a fortnight while he evolved social reasons for the judge's shabby eccentricities, grounding these ultimately in

> his disappointment that the fall of the old rulers had not introduced a new era but merely an era of new ones. hence he goes on practising bourgeois justice, but in a disreputable, sabotaged version which has been made to serve the total self-interest of the judge. this explanation of course mustn't modify what i had in mind, and is for instance to be no excuse for *azdak*.

But this hitch is not reflected in the script. Nor, other than very marginally, is the remodelling of the heroine which another entry of 8 August says has taken him three weeks; he may have found Katya in the first script 'nicer' and not enough like Brueghel's *Dulle Griet* (who is glued on the title-pages of the three earliest scripts), but he does not seem to have altered her much, or provided those practical motives for her goodness which Feuchtwanger (who thought her 'too holy') had asked for. Altogether the changes to his first conception were surprisingly slight.

The first script bears a note by Brecht, 'first version' and is dated 'Santa Monica 5.6.44', the day when he posted it off to Luise Rainer. By August James and Tania Stern had embarked on a rough translation and Auden was prepared to do the verse. Brecht's second script, which contains the new version of the prologue and an *ad lib* epilogue, is similarly headed 'second version'; it must have been finished early in September, and consists very largely of carbons of the first, with some retyped pages. Its title-page gives the names of Eisler and Winge as 'collaborators' as well as that of [Ruth] Berlau who figures alone in the published version; John Hans Winge was an Austrian who had been working in a Los Angeles factory. Both scripts were bound for Brecht, and he seems to have made his amendments, e.g. of names, indifferently in one or the other. These were then taken into a third, undated script of 1944, which would appear to be the version photographed and put into the New York Public Library by Ruth Berlau early in 1945. Like the first two, it was typed by Brecht, but this time using upper- and lower-case letters. The play was first actually published in English, not in the Sterns' version, with Auden's lyrics, but in a new translation by Eric and Maja Bentley which appeared as one of *Two Parables for the Theatre* in 1948. The first German publication was in the special Brecht issue of *Sinn und Form* (Potsdam) the following year. This in turn was amended by Brecht for publication in the *Versuche* series in 1954.

2. SCENE-BY-SCENE ACCOUNT

The following are scene-by-scene notes on the main differences:

1. *The Struggle for the Valley*

In all three scripts and the *Sinn und Form* version this was called 'Prologue', and perhaps as a result many critics and directors have taken it as not forming an integral part of the play. However, as Brecht pointed out in his letter to his publisher Suhrkamp (p. 104), it forms the beginning of the first script and, though altered, was never thereafter omitted. In that first version, which sets the episode on Sunday, 7 June 1934, there are no references to war damage and the scene is nearly two pages shorter. We reproduce it in full on pp. 124–28. Another early note, which may even have preceded it, specifies:

> *scene:* in the background a school with posters and a soviet flag.
> a few dusty trees.

meeting: the folklore not to be overdone. those present are in their sunday best, no traditional costumes. among them a soldier on leave. a woman has a child on her lap. some of the men have very short haircuts.

the singer wears european garb. very comfortable; like all suits, his is somewhat crumpled. his musicians wear russian shirts; one of them has a georgian cap.

the tone of the discussion is very relaxed; a general delight in argument is evident. now and again one of the young people shoots a paper dart at a girl opposite and is told to shut up.

Within three months the scene had been rewritten virtually in its final form. Only its ending was different, being taken from the first version, from its last stage direction ('While they begin to move off', etc.) to the Voice's closing announcement. This was altered in 1954, after the *Sinn und Form* publication. Another minor point involved the switching of the names of the two collective farms, which was done on the second script but inadvertently overlooked in the *Sinn und Form* version. Here Hanns Eisler performed what he ironically called 'one of my great services to German literature' by telling Brecht that, given the insulting use of the term 'goat' for a woman in Germany (cf. the English 'cow'), he should not identify a goat farm with the name of Rosa Luxemburg.

2. The Noble Child

The scripts all amplify the opening stage direction by the words 'his manner of performing shows that he has done it a hundred times before; he turns the pages mechanically, casting an occasional glance at them. By slight movements he tells the musicians when to come in'. In the first script this ran on . . . 'and prefixes each entry of the actors by striking the ground with a wooden mallet'. See the note in Brecht's journal for 3 July 1944, which argues that the play's successive episodes are 'embodiments of the main incidents in his tale' and pictures him striking the ground thus and behaving like a director at a performance. 'this is necessary to avoid illusion and its intoxicating effects'. This idea is abandoned in number 7 of Brecht's notes above (p. 102).

Aside from the subsequent change of names, which has already been mentioned and which gives a much more Georgian flavour, the amendments to the first script are generally minor ones. The dusty messenger originally entered just before the Governor's 'Not before divine service' (p. 12) which was followed by the exchange 'Did you hear', etc. (p. 14); this was altered only in the 1950s. The references to geese in the dialogue between Grusha (Katya) and Simon (Volodya Surki) were originally to fish, but appear in the second script. Katya's answer to the query 'Is the young lady as healthy as a fish in water' was

> Why as a fish in water, soldier? Why not like a horse at a horse market? Can it pull two carts? Can it stand out in the snow while the coachman gets drunk? Being healthy depends on not being made ill.
>
> SURKI: That won't happen.

—while when he asks if she is impatient and wants apples (not cherries) in winter she retorts 'Why not say "does she want a man before she's too old?"'' This and the new stress on her aptitude for the role of 'sucker' ('You simple soul', 'You're a good soul', 'You're just the kind of fool', p. 23) represent the main differences between Grusha and the Katya of the first script.

Her song 'When you return I will be there' (19) was a response to Konstantin Simonov's war poem 'Wait for Me', whose translation, by Nathalie Rene, Brecht had cut out of *Moscow News* and gummed in his journal at the time of the first work on *Simone Machard*:

> Wait for me and I will come.
> Wait, and wait again.
> Wait where you feel sad and numb
> And dreary in the rain.
> Wait, when snows fall more and more,
> Wait when days are hot . . .

etc., the 'I' of course here being a soldier. The remainder of the verse in this scene is virtually unchanged from the first version, though the 'temptation to do good' there was 'great' and not 'terrible'. It is interesting perhaps that the whole line in its present form should have been very firmly written in by Brecht on the second script; he clearly felt it to be important.

3. The Flight into the Northern Mountains
Much of the unrhymed verse (which was originally not broken into lines but divided by oblique strokes) differs in the first script, where it is mainly struck out without having yet been replaced by

the new versions; maybe these became detached from the script. In the second script it is all there, virtually as now. According to Rudolf Vápeník the song 'O sadly one morning' of the two Iron-shirts on p. 173 is translated from a Moravian folksong set (as one of his Slovak Folk Songs) by Bartók; it could be a by-product of Brecht's researches for *Schweyk*.

The first episode (Grusha getting milk from the old peasant) is one of those which Brecht retyped entirely for the second script, but despite some rewording it was not substantially changed. As revised it ended with the words 'Michael, Michael, I certainly took on a nice burden with you' (p. 27), followed by the stage direction:

> *She stands up, worried, takes the child on her back and marches on. Grumbling, the old man collects his can and looks expressionlessly after her.*

The next episode (In front of the caravansary), which figures in the first script, was then cut, not to be restored till the collected edition; it was not performed in Brecht's production. The brief appearance of the two Ironshirts which follows was slightly bowdlerised in the 1950s; before 'He lets himself be hacked to pieces by his superiors' (p. 33) it read 'When he hears an order he gets a stand; when he sticks his lance into the enemy's guts he comes'. The short scene with the two peasants is virtually unchanged from the first script, but once Grusha runs into the Ironshirts there are a fair number of alterations; the central part of the episode being among the passages retyped by Brecht for the second script. The gist of his changes here is to make Grusha more evidently frightened of the soldiers than was Katya in the first version, and also to make it seem less likely that she is handing the child over to the peasants for good. Thus Katya was not 'frightened' (p. 35) and did not 'utter a little scream' (p. 36)— these directions appearing only from the third script on—while instead the first script made her laugh and say:

> Corporal, if you're going to question me so severely I'll have to tell you the truth: that I'd like to be on my way. How about lowering your lance?

The episode of the bridge is once again almost as in the first script, though there is one possibly significant detail: the First Man originally greeted Katya's feat in exactly the words the First Soldier uses of the similarly-named Kattrin in the drum scene of *Mother Courage* (*Collected Plays*, Vol. 5): 'She's made it'. Brecht changed this in the 1950s to 'She's across', presumably in order not to stress the connection between the two characters, both of whom were at that time played by the same actress, Angelika Hurwicz.

4. *In the northern Mountains*
Originally entitled 'Katya Grusha's sojourn at her cowardly brother's: her strange marriage and the return of the soldier'. A number of passages here were retyped and rewritten for the second script, for instance the episode of the melting snow, starting with the Singer's introduction (p. 45):

THE SINGER
The sister was too ill. The cowardly brother had to shelter her / She lay in the store room. Through the thin wall she heard him talking to his wife: / 'She'll soon be gone', he said. 'When she's well. How soft your breasts are . . .'. / The sister was ill till winter came. The cowardly brother had to shelter her. / The store room grew cold and she heard him talk to his wife. / 'When spring comes she'll be gone', he said. 'How firm your thighs are . . .'. / The room was cold. The road was colder. The winter was long, the winter was short. / The rats must not bite, the child must not cry, the spring must not come. / *Where to go when the snow melts?*
Still weak, Katya squats at the loom in the store room. She and the child, who is squatting on the ground, are wrapped in rugs and rags against the cold. The child cries. Katya tries to comfort it. [At this point there is a photograph of a Mongolian-looking woman at a spinning-wheel gummed into the script.]
KATYA: Don't cry, or do it quietly. Otherwise my sister-in-law will hear us and we'll have to go. Cockroaches aren't supposed to make any noise, are they? If we keep as quiet as cockroaches they'll forget we're in the house. Remember the cockroaches. *The child cries again.* Hush. The cold doesn't have to make you cry. Being poor's one thing, freezing's another. It doesn't get you liked. You keep quiet and I'll let you see the horses; remember the horses. *The child cries again.* Michael, we have to be clever, we've no wedding lines for my sister-in-law. If we make ourselves small we can stay till the snow melts. *She draws the child to her and looks, appalled, at one particular point.* Michael, Michael, you've got no sense. If it's on account of the rats you don't need to cry. Rats are quite human. They have families. They store up food for 500 years.

PIOTR *slips in:* What's up? Why are you looking over at that corner, Katya? Is he frightened?
KATYA: What's he to be frightened of? There's nothing there.
PIOTR: I thought I heard scuffling in the straw. I hope it isn't rats. You wouldn't be able to stay with the child here.
KATYA: There aren't any rats. It'd be impossible to get a job anywhere with him.
PIOTR *sits by her:* I wanted to talk to you about Lisaveta . . .

Piotr is Lavrenti, and Lisaveta his wife Aniko, and the conversation continues much as in our text from 'She has a good heart' to 'Was I talking about Aniko?' (pp. 46–7), then:

> You can't think how it upsets her not to be able to offer you anything better than this room. The big room above is too hard to heat. 'My sister will understand': I've told her that a thousand times, but does she believe me? She even blames herself privately for not being able to stand children. That's because she hasn't any of her own. Her heart's not strong enough, you see.

Grusha's song 'Then the lover started to leave' (p. 46) then comes after the second 'Grusha is silent' (p. 47). After the 'beat of the falling drops' (ditto) Piotr makes his proposal about the marriage, much as in our text except that Katya is to come back to live in his house again as soon as her bridegroom dies; the provision about her being allowed to stay on in the latter's farm for two years (p. 49) only appearing in the third script. The wedding ceremony itself was hardly changed except in this respect, thus on leaving (p. 50) Piotr/Lavrenti says 'I'll wait for you by the poplar at the entrance to the village, Katya'.

KATYA: Suppose it takes longer?
MOTHER-IN-LAW: It won't take longer.

The conversation among the guests (p. 53) was retyped vitually as now for the second script; in the first it ran:

> THE GUESTS *noisily:* There've been more disturbances in the city, have you heard?—Ay, the boyar Rajok's besieged in the palace, they say.—The Grand Duke is back and it's all going to be like it used to be.—Lots of them coming back all the time from the Persian war.—They even say the old governor's wife's come back, and all the palace guard with her. *Katya drops the baking sheet. People help her to pick up the cakes.*

A WOMAN *to Katya:* You not feeling well? Too much excite-
ment, that's it. Sit down and have a rest. *Katya sits down.*
THE GUESTS: Here today, gone tomorrow. Gone tomorrow,
here today. But we still have to pay taxes.
KATYA *feebly:* Did someone say the palace guard had come
back?
A MAN: That's what I heard.
ANOTHER: They say, though, that boyar Rajok's green flag is
still flying over the palace. But the palace is being besieged.
The old governor's wife is supposed to be living in one of the
houses opposite.
KATYA: Who told you that?
THE MAN *to a woman:* Show her your shawl . . .

Thenceforward (p. 53) to the end of the scene the first version
has been altered very little, the one significant addition (on the
second script) being Grusha's explanation that she cannot go back
to Nukha (originally Kachezia) because she had knocked down an
Ironshirt.

5. The Story of the Judge
Most of the amendments to this scene are minor ones, and a good
few date from 1954; the three scripts are thus close to one another,
only the episode with the Fat Prince's nephew having been to
some extent rewritten after the first script. Already there the
Singer, who up to that point had only figured as such, began from
the beginning of the Azdak ballad on p. 73 to be 'The Singer
together with his musicians', and this is oddly enough the only
hint anywhere in the play or Brecht's notes that he may be required
to perform Azdak's part, though Brecht seems to have taken this
for granted in the production.

The Ironshirts' action in dragging Azdak to the gallows was
added in 1954; previously they had been slapping him and
Schauva genially on the shoulder. The Fat Prince's (the boyar
Rajok's) first speech was altered and expanded in the rewriting
for the second script; at the same time the chatter of the Ironshirts (p. 69) emphasizing their awareness of their (momentary)
political importance was also added. Some small changes were
made to heighten the dialogue where the Nephew pronounces his
verdict (p. 71), both in the rewriting and in 1954. After the
first two of Azdak's cases (respectively the doctor and Ludovica)
the stage direction showing Azdak on his travels (p. 77) along the

Military Highway and the two accompanying verses of the Azdak ballad were introduced in 1954. The presence of Ironshirts behind Azdak's throne each time, with their flag as a tangible sign of support for him, was an addition on the first script, as was also the appearance of the Fat Prince's head on one of their lances (p. 80).

6. *The Chalk Circle*

In the first script there is a song near the beginning of the scene (after the Cook starts praying, p. 83) which was thereafter omitted:

> SINGER *softly:*
> The people say: the poor need luck
> They won't get far by using their heads.
> They won't grow fat by the work of their hands.
> Therefore, it is said
> God has devised for them games of chance
> And the dog races. Likewise God
> In his unremitting care for his poor folk
> See to it that the tax inspectors sometimes slip.
> For the poor need luck.

All through there are two elements missing from this version—the threat which the wounded corporal represents to Grusha, and Simon's confession that he is the father of the child. Instead Simon alleges that it was the son of one of his comrades. Then after the entry of the Governor's Wife, the First Lawyer goes on from his condemnation of the judges as 'about the lowest' (p. 86) to say

> I insist you settle this matter out of court.
> GOVERNOR'S WIFE: As you wish.
> FIRST LAWYER: In view of the size of the estate which the child is inheriting, what do a few piastres count here and there? *On a nod from her he strolls over to Katya:* A thousand piastres. *Seeing Katya's look of uncertainty:* I am authorized to offer you a thousand piastres if the case can be kept from coming to court.
> THE COOK: Holy Mary, a thousand piastres!
> FIRST LAWYER *strutting off:* You see what your friends think.
> KATYA: Are they trying to offer me money for Michael?
> THE COOK: And they'd certainly go higher.

VOLODYA *darkly:* A meal that doesn't fill you makes you hungry, they say.

FIRST LAWYER *coming back:* Well, what about that thousand?

GOVERNOR'S WIFE: Is she being brazen enough to think it over? *Crosses to Katya:* You shameless person, don't you know you've to bow when I speak to you?

KATYA *bows deeply, then:* I can't sell him, Milady.

GOVERNOR'S WIFE: What? You call that selling, when you've got to return what you stole? You thief, you know it's not yours!

VOLODYA *sees Katya hesitating; at attention:* I attest that this is the child of my comrade Illo Toboridze, Mrs Anastasia Sashvili, sir.

GOVERNOR'S WIFE: Aren't you one of the palace guard? How dare you lie to me, you swine?

VOLODYA: Straight from the horse's mouth, sir, as the saying goes. *The Governor's Wife is speechless.*
Ironshirts have entered the courtyard and the Adjutant has been whispering to one of them. The Second Lawyer tugs the Governor's Wife's sleeve and whispers something to her.

THE COOK: They wouldn't be offering money if they weren't frightened of Azdak's favouring you. He goes by faces.

All this was dropped in the second script, which contained the present short bridge passage to cover the cut.

The first part of the actual hearing, up to Simon's testimony, was retyped after the first script, everything between Grusha's 'He's mine' (p. 88) and the middle of the Second Lawyer's speech beginning 'Thanks, Your Worship' (p. 89) being new. Originally Grusha was followed by the Second Lawyer saying

Excuse me, Maxim Maximovitch, but the court wants facts. My lord, . . .

FIRST LAWYER: My dear Pavlov Pavlovitch, I would have thought my address . . .

SECOND LAWYER: Is dispensable, my dear Maxim Maximovitch. My lord, by an unfortunate chain of circumstances, this child, [etc.]

This means that all reference to the Abashvili (or Sashvili) estates was lacking from the original scene, since the same is true of their mention in the Second Lawyer's speech later on p. 95. Much of the backchat between Azdak and Grusha likewise comes from the

second script, which first introduced Grusha's long diatribe
starting 'You drunken onion' (p. 92) and ending 'than swinging
from the gallows' (below). Her passage too with the Governor's
Wife (p. 94) is a product of that script, but from then on till the
final dance the first version has survived very largely intact. It
ends with the Singer's final verses in a slightly different line
arrangement, and without the ironic qualifying word 'almost',
which was an addition to the second script. An epilogue follows,
but was evidently written later; its use was to be optional, and it is
not included in the third script or any of the published versions
other than the *Materialien zu Brechts 'Der kaukasische Kreidekreis'*
(Suhrkamp-Verlag, Frankfurt, 1966), from which the following
translation has been drawn:

EPILOGUE
(*ad libitum*)

*The ring of spectators from the two collective farms becomes visible.
There is polite applause.*

PEASANT WOMAN RIGHT: Arkady Tcheidse, you slyboots,
   friend of the valley-thieves, how dare you compare us members of the Rosa Luxemburg collective with people like that
   Natella Abashvili of yours, just because we think twice about
   giving up our valley?
SOLDIER LEFT *to the old man right, who has stood up:* What are
   you looking over there for, comrade?
THE OLD MAN RIGHT: Just let me look at what I'm to give
   up. I won't be able to see it again.
THE PEASANT WOMAN LEFT: Why not? You'll be coming
   to call on us.
THE OLD MAN RIGHT: If I do I mayn't be able to recognize
   it.
KATO THE AGRONOMIST: You'll see a garden.
THE OLD MAN RIGHT *beginning to smile:* May God forgive
   you if it's not one.
They all get up and surround him, cheering.

3. PROLOGUE FROM THE FIRST SCRIPT (1944)

*Public square of a Caucasian market town, with peasants and tractor
drivers of two collectivized villages seated in a circle, smoking and
drinking wine; among them a delegate from the planning commission in
the capital, a man in a leather jacket. There is much laughter.*

THE DELEGATE *in an effort to get their attention:* Let's draw up an agreed statement, comrades.

AN OLD PEASANT *standing:* It's too soon for that, I'm against it; we haven't thrashed things out; I object on scientific grounds.

WOMAN'S VOICE *from the right:* Not thrashed it out? We've been arguing ten hours.

THE OLD PEASANT: And what about it, Tamara Oboladze? We've still got four hours left.

A SOLDIER: Correct. I'm surprised at you, Tamara. Who's going to get up from table when there's still a quarter of a calf left in the dish? Who's going to be satisfied with ten hours of argument if he can have fourteen?

A GIRL: We've done Cain and Abel, but nobody's even mentioned Adam and Eve yet. *Laughter.*

THE DELEGATE: Comrades, my head's in a whirl. *Groaning:* All this elaborate business about scientifically based goat breeding, all those examples to back it, all those subtle allusions, and then great masses of goat's cheese and endless jugs of wine to top it off! I suggest we close the discussion, comrades.

A TRACTOR DRIVER *decisively:* Even the best things must come to an end. Hands up those who want the discussion closed! *The majority raise their hands.*

THE TRACTOR DRIVER: The closure's carried. Now for the statement!

THE DELEGATE: The point at issue then *he begins writing in his notebook* is a difference between two collective farms, the Rosa Luxemburg and Galinsk, concerning a valley which lies between them and is not much good for grazing. It belongs to the Rosa Luxemburg collective *addressing those stage left of him* and is being claimed by the Galinsk collective, *to those stage right of him,* that's you people.

THE OLD MAN: Put down that we have to have the valley for raising our goats, just like we have to have other valleys, and it's always belonged to our village. *Applause left.*

A PEASANT RIGHT: What d'you mean, 'always'? Nothing's 'always' belonged to anybody. You haven't even always belonged to yourself. Twenty-five years ago, Chachava, you still belonged to the Grand Duke. *Applause left.*

THE DELEGATE: Why don't we say the valley belongs to you now?

THE PEASANT RIGHT: And when you say you have to have it for your goats, better put in that you've plenty more pasture land not more than half an hour from there.

A WOMAN LEFT: Put this down. If goats are driven half an hour every day they give less milk.

THE DELEGATE: Please don't let's go through all that again. You could have government aid to build stables on the spot.

THE OLD MAN LEFT: I'd like to ask you *addressing the Peasant Right* a small personal question. Did you or did you not enjoy our goat's-milk cheese? *On his not immediately replying:* Did you or did you not enjoy those four or five pounds you were tucking away? I'd like an answer, if you don't mind.

THE PEASANT RIGHT: The answer's yes. So what?

THE OLD MAN *triumphantly:* I wonder if the comrade knows why he enjoyed our goat's-milk cheese? *Pause for effect.* Because our goats enjoyed the grass in that particular valley. Why isn't cheese just any old cheese, eh? Because grass isn't just any old grass. *To the Delegate:* Put that in your book. *Laughter and applause right.*

THE DELEGATE: Comrades, this isn't getting us anywhere.

THE PEASANT RIGHT: Just write down why we think the valley ought to be made over to us. Mention our expert's report on the irrigation scheme, then let the Planning Commission make up its mind.

THE DELEGATE: The comrade agronomist!
A girl stands up right.

NATASHA: Put me down as Nina Meladze, agronomist and engineer, comrade.

THE DELEGATE: Your native village of Galinsk sent you to technical school in Tiflis to study, is that right? *She nods.* And on getting back you worked out a project for the kolkhoz?

NATASHA: An irrigation scheme. We've a lake up in the mountains that can be dammed so as to irrigate 2000 versts of barren soil. Then our kolkhoz can plant vines and fruit trees there. It's a project which can only be economic if the contested valley is included. The yield of the land will go up 6000 per cent. *Applause right.* It's all worked out here, comrade. *She hands him a file.*

THE OLD MAN LEFT *uneasily:* Put in a word to say that our kolkhoz thinks of going in for horse breeding, will you?

THE DELEGATE: Gladly. I think I've got it all now. There's just one more suggestion I'd like to make if I may, comrades.

It would please me very much if I could add a footnote to my report saying that the two farms have come to an agreement after having heard all the arguments put forward this day, Sunday June 7th 1934.

General silence.

THE OLD MAN LEFT *tentatively:* The question is, who does the valley belong to? Why don't we have another drink or two and talk it over? There are still some hours to go. . . .

THE PEASANT RIGHT: All right, let's take our time over the footnote, but do let's close the discussion as decided, specially as it's holding up our drinking eh, comrades?

Laughter.

VOICES: Yes, close the discussion. How about a bit of music?

A WOMAN: The idea was to round off this visit by the Planning Commission's delegate by listening to the singer Arkadi Cheidze. We've been into it with him. *While she is speaking a girl runs off to fetch the singer.*

THE DELEGATE: That sounds interesting. Thank you very much, comrades.

THE OLD MAN LEFT: But this is off the point, comrades.

THE WOMAN RIGHT: Not really. He got in this morning, and promised he'd perform something which had a bearing on our discussion.

THE OLD MAN LEFT: That'd be different. They say he's not at all bad.

THE PEASANT RIGHT *to the Delegate:* We had to telegraph to Tiflis three times to get him. It nearly fell through at the last minute because his chauffeur caught a cold.

THE WOMAN RIGHT: He knows 21,000 verses.

THE PEASANT RIGHT: It's very difficult to book him. You people in the Planning Commission ought to see he comes north more often, comrade.

THE DELEGATE: I'm afraid we're mainly involved with economics.

THE PEASANT RIGHT *with a smile:* You sort out the distribution of grapes and tractors; why not songs too? Anyhow here he is.

Led by the girl, the singer Arkadi Cheidze enters the circle, a thick-set man with simple manners. He is accompanied by four musicians with their instruments. Applause greets the artists.

THE GIRL *introducing them:* This is the comrade delegate, Arkadi.

THE DELEGATE *shakes his hand:* It is a great honour to meet you. I heard about your songs way back as a schoolboy in Moscow. Are you going to give us one of the old legends?

THE SINGER: An extremely old one. It's called 'The Chalk Circle' and comes from the Chinese. We perform it in a somewhat altered version of course. Comrades, it's a great honour for me to entertain you at the end of your day of strenuous debates. We hope that you'll find the old poet's voice doesn't sound too badly under the shadow of Soviet tractors. Mixing one's wines may be a mistake, but old and new wisdom mix very well. I take it we're all having something to eat before the performance begins? It's a help, you know.

VOICES: Of course. Everyone into the club.

As they disperse the Delegate turns to the girl.

THE DELEGATE: I hope it won't finish too late. I have to go home tonight, comrade.

THE GIRL *to the Singer:* How long will it take, Arkadi? The comrade delegate has got to get back to Tiflis tonight.

THE SINGER *offhandedly:* A matter of hours.

THE GIRL *very confidentially:* Couldn't you make it shorter?

THE SINGER *seriously:* No.

VOICE: When you've finished eating, Arkadi Cheidze will give his performance out here on the square.

All go off to eat.

[From Werner Hecht (ed.): *Materialien zu Brechts 'Der kaukasische Kreidekreis'.* Suhrkamp-Verlag, Frankfurt, 1966. This comes from the first script of the play, which was finished by June 1944. The inconsistency in the girl agronomist's name (which is Kato in the final version) is due to its being Georgianized from Natasha Borodin in course of many similar amendments to this script. It may be relevant to both date and setting of this Prologue that Brecht saw something of the writer O. M. Graf during 1944 in New York. Graf had visited the Caucasus with Tretiakoff and others in 1934.]